STUCK IN THE MIDDLE

STUCK

DISSENTING VIEWS OF WINNIPEG

IN THE

PHOTOGRAPHS BY Bryan Scott | **TEXT BY** Bartley Kives | **FOREWORD BY** John K. Samson

MIDDLE

Great Plains Publications

345-955 Portage Avenue
Winnipeg, Manitoba R3G 0P9
www.greatplains.mb.ca

Great Plains Publications gratefully
acknowledges the financial support
provided for its publishing program by
the Government of Canada through the
Canada Book Fund; the Canada Council
for the Arts; the Province of Manitoba
through the Book Publishing Tax Credit
and the Book Publisher Marketing Assistance
Program; and the Manitoba Arts Council.

Design & Typography by
Relish New Brand Experience

Printed in Canada by Friesens

Library and Archives
Canada Cataloguing in Publication

Scott, Bryan, 1974-, photographer
   Stuck in the middle : dissenting views
   of Winnipeg / photos by Bryan Scott;
   text by Bartley Kives.

Includes bibliographical references and index.
ISBN 978-1-926531-84-7 (pbk.)

1. Winnipeg (Man.)—Pictorial works.
2. Winnipeg (Man.)—Social conditions—
21st century. I. Kives, Bartley,
writer of added commentary

II. Title.

FC3396.37.S26 2013   971.27'43040222
C2013-904602-X

MIX
Paper from
responsible sources
FSC® C016245
FSC
www.fsc.org

ENVIRONMENTAL BENEFITS STATEMENT

Great Plains Publications saved the following
resources by printing the pages of this book on
chlorine free paper made with 10% post-consumer
waste.

TREES	WATER	ENERGY	SOLID WASTE	GREENHOUSE GASES
2	**977**	**1**	**66**	**180**
FULLY GROWN	GALLONS	MILLION BTUs	POUNDS	POUNDS

Environmental impact estimates were made using the Environmental Paper Network
Paper Calculator 3.2. For more information visit www.papercalculator.org.

FOR JENNIFER AND KATARINA

FOREWORD

I discovered Bryan Scott's work for the first time at his website winnipeglovehate.com, where he posts his evocative, original photos of Winnipeg's buildings and landmarks. I promptly set it in the context of two of the best known photographers who've taken the city of Winnipeg as their primary theme: L.B. Foote, that great observer of Winnipeg's adolescence, who recorded both the events and construction sites that still frame this place; and John Paskievich, who unflinchingly documented the sixties and seventies of the North End, the abiding philosophical heart of the city, vibrant and neglected, pulse of our precarious hopes.

Bryan Scott's photos certainly document and explore Winnipeg, but they also have this unique trick of swinging open to the viewer, welcoming them in. While acknowledging the obvious, that they are technically accomplished and beautifully composed, I've always been struck most by the fact that Bryan's photos generally lack human figures. I think this lets the photos build a stage, a proscenium arch for viewers to not only peer through, but also climb into and place themselves upon. We're given permission to inhabit the scenes Bryan has created, and something liberating and fundamentally democratic occurs as we experience the subjects as truly ours: our shared streets and buildings, our common incredible sky.

Scott's photos often determined absence of humans encourages us to consider what our buildings are without us, what an empty street says. They remind us that our time here is brief, and might be made more meaningful through the attempt to understand where we are.

Like other great photographers, Bryan Scott's work seems to voice the essential and too often stifled demand, "tell me a story." Bartley Kives, who has always endeavored to illuminate the city of Winnipeg in his writing, is the ideal person to respond. Bart's prose, honed by decades of conscientious and emphatic journalism, is always assured and bright. His concerns and affections are constantly spilling outside the boundaries of his multiple job titles, which have included (but are never limited to) music writer, city hall reporter, epicure and environmentalist.

Working with Scott's photos gives Kives an opportunity to use an isolated prairie city, a potentially dismal and narrow theme, to speak about his remarkably diverse and eclectic concerns. And he does so in what I hear as a uniquely Winnipeg voice: caring and caustic, insightful and wry.

This book is a remarkable collaboration of experts in the field of Winnipeg. Kives and Scott, with vigorous skepticism and nearly pathological affection, have made a hilarious, instructive and beautiful gift for this bewildering city. This place we love and hate and are lucky to call home.

John K. Samson

CONTENTS

1

STUCK
IN THE
MIDDLE

For the sake of an exercise, pretend you're a god. You can go anywhere you want, by any mode of transportation you desire. What you're most likely to desire is to travel as far away as possible from the coastlines of the continents, where the vast majority of humanity resides. This is a logical desire, as all gods consider homo sapiens a nuisance, if not a pest species.

Vancouver sculptor Bill Pechet pretty much nailed Winnipeg when he came up with the concept for emptyful, an LED-illuminated, stainless-steel fountain installed at Millennium Library Park in 2012. The Erlenmeyer flask is intended to be a "symbolic container of emptiness" that evokes the wide-open spaces of the prairies — and ask the eternal question about whether a bottle is half empty or half full.

In geographic terms, they call such a place a pole of inaccessibility — the farthest location you can travel from any coast. In Eurasia, discriminating deities will wind up in the Gurbantünggüt Desert, an arid patch of western China's Xinjiang province, a few kilometres from the Kazakh border. In South America, misanthropic multidimensional beings may escape to the savannahs of the Mato Grosso plateau to enjoy the quiet company of Brazilian cattle. In Africa, the ultimate escape will place you among the pigeons and parrots of the Bengangai Game Reserve, near the tri-border confluence of South Sudan, the Central African Republic and the Democratic Republic of the Congo.

In North America, however, the farthest place from anywhere is already occupied — by Winnipeg, home to more than 700,000 people and zero gods. More than any other city on the continent, Winnipeg is stuck in the middle.

Head east from Winnipeg in a car and it's a 2,700-kilometre drive to the Gulf of St. Lawrence, which flows into the Atlantic Ocean in the general vicinity of Riviere-du-Loup. This coastal Quebec town is the birthplace of Alexandre-Antonin Taché, the first Archbishop of St. Boniface, a Cassandra figure who tried and failed to prevent the 1870 Métis unrest that established Manitoba and paved the way for Winnipeg to be a provincial capital.

Drive west from Winnipeg and it's 2,300 kilometres to the Pacific coast city of Vancouver, a railway terminus whose early growth originally mirrored that of the Manitoba capital, once Canada's biggest railway hub. But after the 1914 completion of the Panama Canal, the Port of Vancouver became a more profitable shipping route and Gastown assumed Winnipeg's role as western Canada's most important city.

Drive south from Winnipeg and it's 2,750 kilometres to Corpus Christi, a Texas city on the Gulf of Mexico. Visit the suburb of Flour Bluff, and you may find yourself at the corner of Winnipeg Drive and Manitoba Drive, where a series of nondescript bungalows pay homage to hopelessly bored Prairie-dwellers who actually did get in their cars and drive until they could not go any further.

You cannot travel by car directly from Winnipeg to the Arctic Ocean. But it's only a 1,700 kilometre train ride to Churchill, Manitoba's seaport on Hudson Bay. The Scottish settlers who helped found the Red River settlement that would eventually spawn Winnipeg had to travel through the vast emptiness of Hudson Bay, whose shores are patrolled by polar bears. Open up a Lonely Planet guide to Canada and you will find as many pages devoted to Churchill as there are to Winnipeg. In the eyes of international tourists, the permafrozen tundra is more attractive than a city that simply has the reputation of being among the coldest in the world.

If you insist on technicality, the North American pole of inaccessibility actually is embedded in the South Dakota badlands. But Winnipeg has more than just geographic reasons to claim the continent's extreme centre.

As a city of 700,000, Winnipeg is too small to be cosmopolitan but too large to be folksy. Big-city complaints about violent crime compete with small-town gripes about the absence of privacy and if you're single, a terribly shallow gene pool. Major amenities such as NHL hockey are balanced off by a minor-league transportation network saddled with only a rudimentary rump of a rapid-transit system.

Far from the moderating influence of the seas, Winnipeg is subject to a highly variable, midcontinental climate, where winters are frigid, summers are steamy and both

The north end of Westview Park, a former city landfill, housed a D.I.Y. indie-rock festival called Corefest in the 1990s. The slope makes for a decent toboggan run. Many Winnipeggers just call the place Garbage Hill.

spring and fall can involve either extreme. The annual mean temperature of 2.6° C belies the 81-degree spread between the city's hottest and coldest recorded temperatures.

Winnipeg also falls smack in the middle when it comes to economic growth, chugging along at a modest pace during the entire postwar period while almost everywhere else underwent rapid expansions and precipitous declines. Winnipeg's eggs are divided among many economic baskets — transportation, manufacturing, insurance, food-processing — as if the gods designed a living embodiment of a balanced stock portfolio.

But none of this speaks to the real manner in which Winnipeg is stuck in the middle: it is a city that inspires a profound sense of ambivalence among its residents.

This has nothing to do with apathy, as there's no such thing as a Winnipegger without a strong opinion about the city. They either despise it or adore it, depending on the nanosecond and whether or not the bus came on time, the street happened to get plowed or the Blue Bombers won the previous night. While ambivalence of this sort is present in any city, only in Winnipeg does it serve as the defining character of the populace.

In many ways, Winnipeg is a fascinating place. It was born of an act of violent resistance, a unique occurrence in this country. It was the fastest-growing city in North America for a time. It was the site of one of the largest workers' revolts in the western world. It was threatened with destruction by floodwaters twice in half a century. It is the second-smallest city on the continent to boast a major-league professional sports team. It boasts a selection of architectural wonders that range from surviving railway-boom warehouses to twentieth century modernist buildings to a handful of hypermodernist structures.

Yet Winnipeg is also the very vision of homogeneity and inefficiency. It's a low-density city that can barely afford to maintain its sprawling, aging infrastructure. It is not overly walkable or pedestrian-friendly. It makes artistic decisions based on politics and political decisions that appear to be inspired by Dadaism more than any political philosophy. It has a disturbing tendency to allow property owners to neglect and eventually demolish heritage structures.

Winnipeg tends to infuriate Winnipeggers, who sometimes question why they live in the city. But when they consider the alternative, they dare not dream of living anywhere else. Even Winnipeggers who do depart for Toronto, Calgary or Vancouver never assimilate or fully lose their regional identity. They remain stuck on their birthplace, in the middle of the flat, snowy, buggy, flood-prone and isolated prairie, where everyone seems to know everyone despite the impossibility of the arithmetic involved.

To add another onion layer to this already tired analogy, Winnipeg is also stuck in the middle of two possible destinies. One involves maturation into a medium-sized city that learns to live within its means by choosing to reinvigorate its inner core, increase the density of its older neighbourhoods and build new residential areas that make financial and environmental sense.

The other is a slide back to mediocrity by conducting postwar development business as usual: the endless construction of new single-family homes, sprawling out into a distance where the roads and sewers and water pipes will never be as good as the day they are laid, because no future government will be able to maintain them.

Winnipeg is a city on the precipice of a momentous decision, one that really amounts to the cumulative result of a series of smaller decisions. For now, it stands between two futures and potentially many more. Pray to whatever deity you like to ensure the right choices get made. ◼

Come on down to Princess Street for your free estimate.

ABOVE / Easily one of the prettiest venues in minor-league baseball, Shaw Park is snuggled between Waterfront Drive and CN Rail's mainline. A seat in the stands offers a view of the Red River, Esplanade Riel and the Canadian Museum for Human Rights. Outfielders get to see downtown's skyline. The ballpark was built in 1999 for $15 million, with $8.8 million coming from the public purse.

LEFT / Nutty Club is not just a brand name, but a case of truth in advertising for the City of Winnipeg. Everything you need to know about downtown Winnipeg is visible in this frame: Rail lines, surface-parking lots, heritage warehouses and a small clutch of modern office towers.

On Main Street, the weight of the world is borne on the shoulders of just one man.

Roslyn Court, one of Winnipeg's first luxury apartment buildings, arose at the corner of Osborne Street and Roslyn Road in 1909. The red brick and limestone structure continues to serve as the gateway to Osborne Village.

For nearly two decades, motorists driving north over the Slaw Rebchuk Bridge were greeted by the sign on the roof of Nepon Autobody. The business insisted it had nothing to do with the "people before profit" line, claiming the slogan was the work of vandals who intended it as sarcasm. It was removed during roof-maintenance work in 2011.

WELCOME TO
THE NORTH END
PEOPLE BEFORE PROFIT

In Winnipeg's Exchange District, century-old warehouse buildings advertise products that no longer exist. This view is from King Street.

Manitoba Hydro's Portage Avenue headquarters, completed in 2009, marked the return of ambitious architecture to downtown Winnipeg. The $283-million, 22-storey structure is considered one of the most energy-efficient large buildings in the world.

An illuminated Manitoba Legislature marks Winnipeg's 25th Pride celebrations.
The Manitoba capital was the first large city in North America to elect an openly
gay mayor, Glen Murray, in 1998. He resigned after six years to make an
unsuccessful run for federal office.

LEFT / In 1895, hardware magnate James Ashdown, one of the most influential people in Winnipeg's history, built a massive warehouse along Bannatyne Avenue in the East Exchange. In 1988, it was among the first warehouses in Winnipeg to be converted into residential apartments.

BELOW / The sun always shines on the Commodity Exchange Tower — but can not penetrate the depths of its subterranean sister, Winnipeg Square.

RIGHT / Rae & Jerry's Steak House on Portage Avenue has barely changed since 1957. Inside, you'll find dark red walls, wood paneling and a menu that offers a choice of soup or tomato juice as a first course.

A single storey is all that remains of Main Street's Duffin Block, a mixed-use structure that stood three storeys when it was completed in 1882. The block was damaged by a 1904 fire that destroyed James Ashdown's hardware store. Another fire in 1956 destroyed the top two floors. The remaining level was connected to the neighbouring Baker Block and incorporated into Birt's Saddlery. The western-wear retailer sold its final 10-gallon hat in 1995.

In a view of downtown few Winnipeggers ever see, Ellice Avenue, Balmoral Street and
Notre Dame Avenue form an almost perfect triangle, with Central Park embedded in the middle.

ABOVE / November snow becomes fairy dust in Luxton Heights, a North End neighbourhood east of Main Street.

RIGHT / From a vantage point on Taché Avenue, downtown Winnipeg is adorned with mauve waters and a tangerine sky.

20

LEFT / Irish émigré Michael Murphy, who suffered from cognitive impairments after being struck by a car, spent the final years of his life battling addictions on the Main Street strip. The Woodbine Hotel, one of Winnipeg's oldest drinking establishments, is one of the few to survive a two-decade-long city effort to shutter or demolish Main Street hotels. Murphy frequented these hotels, living a Main Street existence while remaining in regular contact with his wife and daughter. He died of a hospital infection in 2010, at the age of 59. His family shared his story after coming across this portrait hanging on the wall of a St. James restaurant.

RIGHT / At twilight, the Red River enlists the willows and cottonwoods in a conspiracy to reclaim the city.

Bison once roamed free across southern Manitoba, sustaining Dakota, Assiniboine and Métis. North America's largest ungulates are capable of sprinting 50 kilometres an hour, which somehow is not fast enough to escape this diorama at the entrance of the Manitoba Museum

2

HANGIN' OUT WITH
LOUIS RIEL

Thirteen thousand years ago, there was nothing at the corner of Portage & Main but a massive blanket of snow and ice. Visit Winnipeg in the middle of January and you might not notice anything has changed.

The story of this city is a tale of glaciation, both in a literal and metaphorical sense. For thousands of years, what's now Winnipeg was buried below ice. Then the glaciers melted, creating room for a city that still exists in a semi-frozen state of suspended animation, awaiting someone or something to thaw it out. But we'll get to that inertia in a bit.

Up until about 11,000 BC, an immense wall of white called the Wisconsin ice sheet completely covered southern Manitoba. The glacier then started receding and expanding in irregular fits and starts, exposing the south-western corner of the province to Manitoba's first human inhabitants and submerging the rest of the south below a big puddle of meltwater called Lake Agassiz.

About 8,000 years ago, the lake finally drained away into Hudson Bay. The first people to visit the newly exposed Agassiz lake bottom — soon to become the Red River Valley — would have encountered little more than an empty expanse of muddy nothingness. Again, you could argue not much has changed.

Over the next few thousand years, the first Manitobans hunted bison and other big furry things, fished for the likes of sturgeon, gathered berries, foraged for wild vegetables and also harvested wild rice. By the early 1400s, some were even farming beans, squash and maize along the Red River.

The first Europeans who arrived in Manitoba encountered Dene in the north, Cree across most of the province, Ojibway in the east and Siouian-speaking Assiniboine in the south. All of this was interesting but initially unimportant to English and French explorers, whose main obsession was to find some form of passage to the Pacific Ocean.

The first white guys to set foot in what's now Winnipeg were explorers from Quebec, encouraged west by rumours of a massive sea in the middle of the continent. That sea turned out to be the large but very shallow Lake Winnipeg, the largest remnant of Lake Agassiz.

The leader of this party was Sieur Pierre Gaultier de la Vérendrye, whose men made their way up the Red River in 1738 and established Fort Rouge near the junction with the Assiniboine River. For the Red River Valley, this marked the beginning of both the fur trade era and a significant European presence. It was also the end of the indigenous way of life in southern Manitoba.

For the first few decades of the fur trade in southern Manitoba, the Francophones had the Fort Rouge area pretty much to themselves. But the Anglos of the Hudson's Bay Company, based at York Factory on the bay itself, were making their way down south to the Red River Valley. Soon the HBC and the Montreal-based North West Company were competing for the same dead animal skins, while their employees were getting busy with the locals.

The resulting effect on the population was profound, as the children of the French and British men who coupled with Cree and Ojibway women became the Métis, the semi-nomadic people who would go on to found the province of Manitoba. During the same period, European diseases such as smallpox and influenza killed off untold numbers of indigenous Manitobans, who had no immunity to the foreign microbes.

While the actual death toll is unknown, it's possible more than 90 per cent of Manitoba's indigenous population succumbed to disease, malnutrition or violence during the first two centuries after Europeans established themselves in the southern reaches of the province. This is a charitable estimate, as well-documented indigenous population losses in other parts of North America exceeded 95 per cent during the same period, mostly due to disease.

On the plus side, Europeans were not quick to make their way to the Red River Valley. In 1809, the North West Company founded Fort Gibraltar within stumbling distance of The Forks. The Hudson's Bay Company responded by building the nearby Fort Douglas in 1812. The same year, HBC investor Lord Selkirk brought a group of settlers over from Scotland to work the rich, black soil of the Red River Valley.

Tensions between the two camps flared up spectacularly in 1816 at The Battle of Seven Oaks, a gunfight between a group of mostly Métis Nor'westers and a smaller band of settlers and HBC men. The death toll was twenty-two, with the HBC/settler side suffering all but one casualty. The two sides essentially spent the next five years threatening to burn down each other's forts.

The fun and games finally ended in 1821, when the two fur-trading outfits merged and renamed their headquarters Upper Fort Garry, just west of The Forks. But the peace and quiet in the Red River Colony was short-lived: in 1826, the greatest flood in Manitoba history submerged the entire Red River Valley, destroying Fort Garry and sending Red River residents scrambling to higher ground in Stony Mountain and Birds Hill, neither of which is really mountainous or hilly.

From a hydrological perspective, there could be no more idiotic place to build a settlement than at the confluence of two frequently flooding prairie rivers, in the middle of a soggy floodplain at the bottom of a former lake. The nomadic Assiniboine and their Cree allies weren't too troubled by frequent deluges; faced with a flood, they would simply ride or walk away. But European settlers, who were fond of surveying plots of land and sticking to them, were traumatized by the 1826 flood and the similar

From 1779 to 1821, the Hudson's Bay Company and the North West Company battled for control of the fur trade in what's now western Canada. Every February, Winnipeggers celebrate this heritage by generally ignoring this lovingly recreated replica of Fort Gibraltar, originally built by Nor'westers in 1810.

1852 event. Swarms of mosquitoes that followed the floods didn't make their stay any more enjoyable.

Nonetheless, the Red River settlement kept growing. At first, both Francophone and English-speaking Métis outnumbered the Scottish settlers and their offspring. But the bison herds were declining, forcing the Métis to abandon the hunting life for a sedentary existence on farms. The arrival of more English-speaking Protestants from Ontario in the 1860s — and some Americans from the south — also changed the character of the settlement.

Out of fear of US expansionism, Canada purchased Rupert's Land, which encompassed most of present-day Manitoba, from the Hudson's Bay Company in 1869. The same year, Ottawa ordered up a survey of the Red River settlement. This angered the Métis, who were scared of losing their ever-more-important farms to new waves of Anglo settlers.

Led by Louis Riel, a skilled orator who was educated in Montreal, the Métis disrupted the survey. They prevented a new Canadian governor from arriving in the area, seized control of Upper Fort Garry and otherwise refused to acquiesce to colonial rule. Riel then formed a provisional government with the intention of entering into negotiations with Ottawa about joining the Dominion of Canada. Even most of the English speakers in the settlement eventually deemed his demands about land and language to be more or less reasonable.

But after a group of Canadians tried to retake the fort, Riel's forces captured forty-six men, shoved them in prison and executed a loud-mouthed character named Thomas Scott. While Riel may have been trying to illustrate he could not be pushed around, killing Scott by firing squad proved to be a big mistake.

Back in Ontario, Protestants were outraged by the execution. Even as Ottawa agreed to make Manitoba Canada's sixth province, federal officials were preparing to remove Riel from power. Manitoba entered into Confederation on July 15, 1870. A month later, a military expedition led by Colonel Garnet Wolseley marched into Winnipeg with the presumed intention of killing Riel. The founder of Manitoba wisely fled before his would-be executioners arrived.

Although he's now considered a hero for his role in the Red River Resistance, Riel was then deemed a traitor and spent most of the next fourteen years in exile, despite being elected to the House of Commons three times. He finally returned to Canada to lead the North-West Rebellion in Saskatchewan, which was crushed under the boot of British and Canadian troops at Batoche in 1885.

Riel was tried for treason in Regina and promptly hanged. His body now rests in Winnipeg on the grounds of the St. Boniface Cathedral, where he once railed against unjust treatment at the hands of Ottawa.

The relatively modest grave belies the fact Louis Riel changed the course of Canadian history. Manitoba remains the only province to be founded by an act of armed resistance, which itself was one of the first instances of a successful campaign for indigenous rights.

In 1873, three years after Manitoba entered into Confederation, Winnipeg was incorporated as a city. One hundred and forty years later, the original tensions plaguing the Red River settlement — over language, land use and indigenous rights — have yet to be resolved.

The glaciers are long gone and Louis Riel is just a dead guy with a mustache. But in many ways Winnipeg remains on ice. ◾

The Selkirk Settlers established the Red River Colony in 1812. What better way to honour these plucky Scots than to plop a sorry-ass statue in the middle of a Waterfront Drive traffic circle, where no sane pedestrian could ever get a close-up glimpse.

RIGHT / To celebrate Manitoba's centennial, sculptor Marcien Lemay and architect Etienne Gaboury teamed up to create this naked and tortured image of Louis Riel — a work of art worthy of the brilliance of Manitoba's founder. Twenty five years later, complaints from mediocre minds led the Filmon government to banish the statue from the grounds of the Manitoba Legislature. It's now hidden behind College Universitaire de Saint-Boniface on Rue Aulneau.

FAR RIGHT / "Look at me, I am a dignified political legend, with actual clothing and an upright posture and a rolled-up copy of the sports section in my hand. Actually, maybe I'm a statue of Peter Falk as Columbo. Why else would I be wearing a trench coat? Now excuse me, I'm about to use this rolled-up newspaper to swat a trio of Osborne Village residential towers." The 1995 Riel statue at the Manitoba Legislature grounds.

There would be no Winnipeg without the railway industry that exploded in the late 19th Century, stagnated in the early 20th and created an urban-revitalization headache in the 21st. The CPR Winnipeg Yards, which have separated the North End from the city's core for 140 years, continue to act as a geopolitical boundary.

The Kay Building, erected on Arthur Street in 1893. Winnipeg's relatively slow growth allowed the city to retain many of the cut-stone and terra cotta warehouse buildings in the Exchange District, much of it protected as a national historic site. Many structures from the late 19th Century and early 20th Century remain in spite of the city's anemic and inconsistent approach to heritage conservation.

RIGHT / During the 1919 General Strike, the Ukrainian Labour Temple on Pritchard Avenue in the North End served as a hangout for the trade unionists and a target for the police. Today, the time-honoured tradition of "salami shoulder" is practiced within its hallowed walls.

BELOW / For a brief period in the early 20th Century, when Winnipeg was the fastest-growing city in North America, every bank in the nation established its own monument. Bankers' Row on Main Street remains a testament to a time when financial institutions deposited more than they withdrew from communities.

FAR RIGHT / Le Market on Rue Des Meurons. Winnipeggers like to boast St. Boniface is the largest francophone neighbourhood in Canada west of the Quebec-Ontario border. Conversely, Winnipeggers like to hide the fact St. Boniface boasts the largest collection of stone heads stacked up on appliances north of Mount Rushmore. Take that, South Dakota.

LEFT / The Lincoln Hotel on McPhillips Street. Winnipeg's fast-growing Filipino population has made Tagalog the second-most-widely-spoken language in the home, behind English and ahead of French. Of North American cities, only San Francisco and San Diego have a higher percentage of residents with roots in the Philippines.

RIGHT / The sun sets on Winnipeg for the 8,100th time since the Blue Bombers won a Grey Cup, the 20,800th time since the last streetcar went for a ride and the 35,700th time since the construction of the Panama Canal stopped the city's growth in its tracks. Optimism yet abounds.

3

ARCHITECTURAL
WONDERS!

In the aftermath of the Red River Resistance, Anglophones and Francophones did their best to get along in the muddy frontier outpost that would soon become the city of Winnipeg. In 1873, when the city was incorporated, it was little more than a series of dirt tracks, wooden homes and a few simple commercial structures, serving a population of 1,869 somewhat nervous and mistrustful souls.

The dominant structure in the city was initially Upper Fort Garry, the birthplace of Manitoba. But it wouldn't be long before the old trading post was considered an inconvenience. Shortly after the railway arrived in town in 1881, most of the old fort was torn to the ground to make way for what's now the southern stretch of Main Street.

The railway's arrival was nothing less than the single most important event in Winnipeg's history. There simply would not be a Winnipeg without the railyards and the tracks that allowed the city to serve as a supply depot for the rest of western Canada.

The 1881 arrival of the railway kicked off a phenomenal, thirty-three-year economic boom. During the first decade after the tracks connected Winnipeg with eastern Canada, the city's population tripled from 9,000 to 27,000. It then leapt almost six-fold over the next twenty years to 150,000 people in 1911.

In 1905, at the pinnacle of the boom, Winnipeg was the fastest-growing city in North America, with a rate of growth outpacing even that of Chicago, its larger railway-boom doppelganger in the heart of the US midwest.

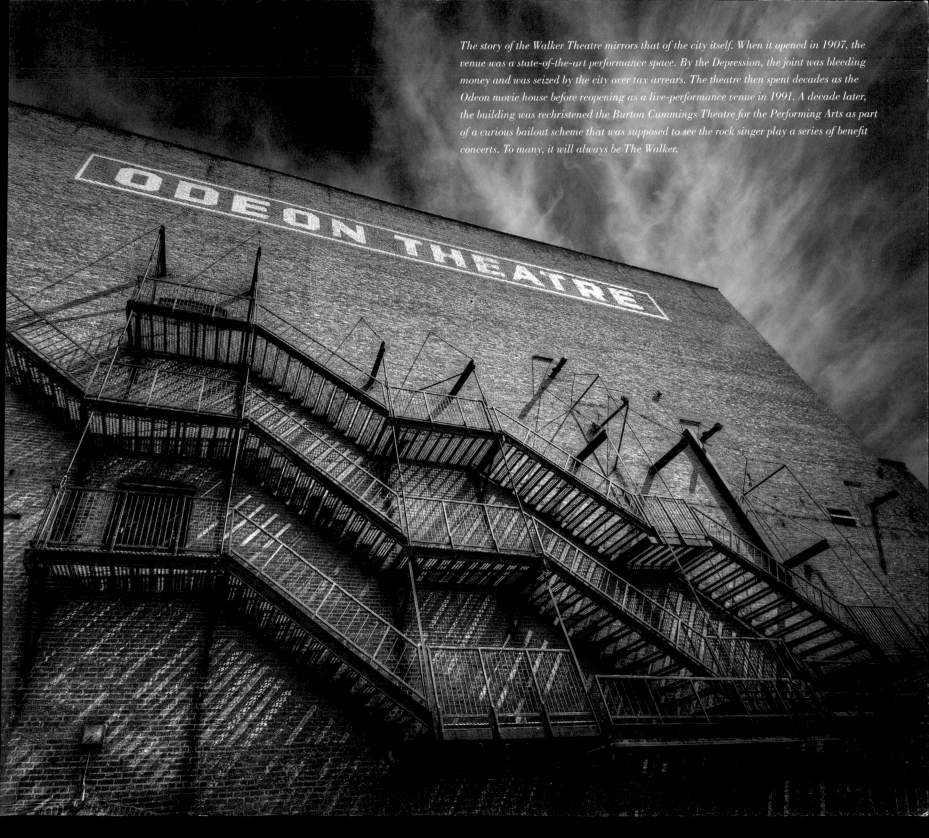

The story of the Walker Theatre mirrors that of the city itself. When it opened in 1907, the venue was a state-of-the-art performance space. By the Depression, the joint was bleeding money and was seized by the city over tax arrears. The theatre then spent decades as the Odeon movie house before reopening as a live-performance venue in 1991. A decade later, the building was rechristened the Burton Cummings Theatre for the Performing Arts as part of a curious bailout scheme that was supposed to see the rock singer play a series of benefit concerts. To many, it will always be The Walker.

Initially, the boom was fuelled by entrepreneurs who imported goods from eastern Canada and shipped them farther west. On either side of Main Street — the initial centre of commerce in the city — merchants built cut-stone warehouses and adorned them with terra cotta facades. Many of these structures still stand in the Exchange District, where enough heritage remains to warrant national historic-site status.

The sudden accumulation of wealth attracted financiers, who built even more ornate bank buildings along Main Street. Neoclassical structures with massive columns, marble floors and sandstone facades sprung up in the new financial district which began spreading west along Portage Avenue, expanding the footprint of the city's commercial core.

The new money also either financed or inspired the construction of the Walker Theatre on Smith Street, the Eaton's department-store complex south of Portage Avenue, the Hotel Fort Garry on Broadway and dozens of other structures that initially inspired awe. By the end of the railway boom, Winnipeg had become Canada's third-largest city, behind only Montreal and Toronto.

Winnipeg was also highly diverse by the standards of the time, thanks to federal immigration policies designed to populate western Canada and discourage American expansionism. By 1911, two in every five Winnipeggers were born outside of Canada, with most of the immigrants coming from Europe. German, Russian, Polish, Ukrainian, Yiddish, Icelandic and Romanian were among the babel of languages spoken in the streets.

There was little integration between the eastern European arrivals and the mostly Anglo-Protestant, nouveau-riche elite. But it didn't matter. The dominant belief at the time was Winnipeg would soon match the economic might of Chicago and emerge as a Canadian midcontinental power.

Little did the locals realize the city's first forty years would be its most triumphant.

In 1914, the completion of the Panama Canal devastated the railway-transport business. Shipping goods by sea turned out to be a heck of a lot cheaper. A full fifteen years before the rest of North America entered the Depression, Winnipeg took a big economic hit. But the full effect was not apparent at the time. The other big event of 1914 had a much more immediate impact.

The start of the First World War led soldiers from Winnipeg to join the large Canadian military contingent in Europe. Factories fired up production to support the war effort, staffed in part by immigrants who picked up the slack from men who left to serve overseas.

When those soldiers returned home in 1918, many found themselves unemployed, as some factories were shutting down and others had no work for them. Industrial conditions also happened to be deplorable, leading workers of all stripes to push for better wages and living conditions. Many organized strikes.

But in the wake of the Russian revolution, Winnipeg's establishment — mostly bankers, employers and politicians — equated the labour-union movement with Bolshevism. They believed the best way to deal with any union was to react as harshly as possible and refuse to negotiate.

Tensions between unions and employers came to a head in the spring of 1919, when almost every worker in Winnipeg walked off the job for six weeks. When the Winnipeg General Strike ended, two union members had been killed in a confrontation with the RCMP, the Winnipeg Free Press had branded all participants as foreign Bolshevists and some strike leaders were convicted for conspiracy and jailed as long as two years.

Main Street's Via Rail Station, ornate interior and all, was built in 1909. A century ago, most visitors to Winnipeg arrived by train. Today, passenger-train travel through the city is little more than an anachronism, favoured only by tourists on cross-country travels or making polar bear-watching pilgrimages to Churchill, way up north on Hudson Bay.

In the aftermath of the strike, the city's economy tanked. The completion of the lavish Manitoba Legislature in 1920 and the construction of the Hudson's Bay Building six years later effectively concluded the golden age of Winnipeg architecture. During the Depression, federal employment programs were required to stimulate construction.

The cure for a sluggish economy proved to be the Second World War, which restored the same degree of optimism to Winnipeg as it did to almost every other North American city. During the postwar boom, the city went on a modernist kick, building funky-yet-functional structures such as the first Great-West Life Building on Osborne Street, the Workers Compensation Building on Broadway, the addition to the Winnipeg Clinic on St. Mary's Avenue and Winnipeg International Airport's heavily design-conscious original terminal.

An entire campus of modernist structures then sprung up on either side of an historic stretch of Main Street, as the city and province started razing entire blocks in the name of downtown revitalization.

First, in the early '60s, the city erected a Civic Centre complex comprised of a block-shaped city hall, a brutalist Public Safety Building and two concrete plazas intended to exist as public space. This was followed late in the decade with the Centennial Centre complex on the other side of Main Street, where the Manitoba Museum, a planetarium and a concert hall continue the concrete theme.

One final spasm of modernist construction erupted in the 1970s in the form of the Winnipeg Art Gallery on Osborne Street, the University of Winnipeg's ultra-industrial Centennial Hall and a space-age pedestrian roundabout buried below the corner of Portage & Main.

By the late '70s, however, the city was practically spent, on both a creative and financial level. Architecture shifted from the whimsical to the purely utilitarian as Winnipeg found itself in decline compared to other Canadian centres.

The 1980s saw a proliferation of pastel-coloured postmodern structures such as the emotionally hollow Portage Place, the centerpiece of a massive multi-government effort to revitalize the north side of Portage Avenue.

More postmodernism appeared at The Forks Market, the first facet of a more successful downtown-revitalization effort — the adaptive reuse of the old railyards at the confluence of the Red and Assiniboine Rivers.

Although The Forks has proven a success, the sum total of all this mega-construction, achieved with the help of more than $1 billion worth of public funds, could not restore life to the city's old commercial core. Decades of postwar suburban expansion left the city decentralized, disconnected and increasingly self-conscious.

By the mid-1990s, downtown Winnipeg seemed desolate and much of the city was distraught by the departure of the Winnipeg Jets to Phoenix. For a generation of young Winnipeggers, the loss of the NHL club represented the symbolic death of a city that once considered itself among the continent's great centres.

But a funny thing happened after the Jets left town in 1996. First, the city was galvanized by a harrowing but successful flood fight in 1997. Then the 1999 Pan Am Games, centred around The Forks, encouraged more Winnipeggers to reacquaint themselves with downtown.

At the dawn of the new millennium, the city grew comfortable within its medium-sized skin. A century after

the canal and the strike, Winnipeg finally began to carve out an identity that had nothing to do with the railway boom.

It also started building interesting structures again, beginning with Esplanade Riel, the priapic pedestrian bridge connecting downtown to St. Boniface. The Manitoba Hydro tower on Portage Avenue, with its solar chimney and automatic windows, is both a monument to provincial hubris and a love letter to environmental design. On Waterfront Drive, the Antoine Predock-designed Canadian Museum for Human Rights threatened to outshine its content, while smaller structures such as The Cube in Old Market Square exemplified the city's willingness to assume risk.

Of course, the bulk of Winnipeg remains the same soulless expanse of fast-food franchises, big-box developments and automotive lots you will find in any other North American city. But interspersed between the prefab horror you will still find traces of every preceding architectural period, preserved by the very same slow growth once damned by the boosters who want to believe we can set back the clock to 1905 and remain that railway boomtown forever. ◼

LEFT / The construction the nine-storey Boyd Building at the corner of Portage Avenue and Edmonton Street in 1912 effectively extended downtown further to the west. Original owner William J. Boyd, an early proponent of urban planning, would have been mortified to learn the building's owners a century later turned an adjacent park into an illegal surface-parking lot and hung an illegal electronic sign from the west side, both in violation of city regulations.

BELOW / Clad in salmon-pink sandstone, the Canada Permanent Building was erected on Garry Street in 1909. Ninety years later, Pan Am Games volunteers would wear the same annoying colour, which looks way better on a building.

FAR LEFT / The McKim Courtyard, built in 1911, is one of the most important structures in Osborne Village, one of Winnipeg's few pedestrian-friendly neighbourhoods. The maze-like interior once housed the original McNally Robinson bookstore.

The DeBary Apartments, now known as the Highgate, has stood watch over the corner of Wardlaw Avenue and Daly Street in Crescentwood since 1913. A large courtyard and many smaller bays and balconies were designed to maximize the penetration of natural light into every apartment.

As imposing today as it was when it was built in 1913, the neo-classical Bank of Montreal building looms over the southeast corner of Portage & Main, serving as a relic from an era when Winnipeggers still dreamed big. Italian marble, bronze and granite all adorn the lovingly maintained interior, where patrons can still feel puny below the 20-metre-high ceiling.

Stories about ghosts gallivanting about the corridors of the Fort Garry Hotel amount to a needless attempt to mystify what's already one of Winnipeg's weirder structures. Built in 1913 as a Grand Trunk Pacific Railway hotel, the Fort Garry originally catered to the luxury crowd. By the 1980s, it was sufficiently down on its luck to sport a punk-rock bar in its basement and an ill-conceived seventh-story casino experiment. An extensive renovation in the '90s allowed the Fort Garry to reclaim its rightful place as the venue of choice for out-of-town wedding guests to hit on each other.

ABOVE / No, it's not a gingerbread house. The Pavilion at Assiniboine Park, built in 1930, is the spiritual centre of Winnipeg's largest public space.

RIGHT / Not to be outdone by audacious opening of the Eaton's building in 1905, the Hudson's Bay Company decided to further expand Winnipeg's downtown footprint by building its own grand flagship store even further west on Portage Avenue in 1926. As this book went to press, The Bay only occupied a few floors of a structure whose future remains very much in doubt.

FAR LEFT / Joanna's Café, on the main floor of Smith Street's Marlborough Hotel, is tucked into the oldest corner of a structure that was only four storeys tall when it opened as the Olympia in 1914. It boasted of being fire-proof, thanks to an interior sprinkler system considered novel at the time.

LEFT / The Manitoba Legislative Building was completed in 1920 after numerous delays resulting from the First World War, labour shortages and even the theft of construction materials by the contractor. The massive building is adorned with references to Greek, Roman, Assyrian, Babylonian and Egyptian mythology, as well as Hebrew and Christian scripture. The arcane knowledge required to balance a budget, however, remains beyond the understanding of the building's current inhabitants. This is a view of the rotunda.

RIGHT / The seven-storey stone Federal Building rose on Main Street in 1935, at the height of The Depression, as part of a City of Winnipeg unemployment-relief program. Today, we would call this infrastructure-stimulus spending. Back then, it was desperately needed work.

The tiers along the Winnipeg Clinic evoke the skyscrapers from The Jetsons, the retro-futuristic cartoon series. In fact, many Winnipeggers just call it the Jetsons Building. The original structure was only two storeys when it was placed on St. Mary Avenue in 1942. The tiers were added as part of a 1959 expansion.

If you ever get bored, drive down Manitoba Avenue to the Polish Gymnastic Association and imagine how athletes who fail to make the grade get impaled upon its spikes. In reality, each antenna is a direct connection to North Korea.

We love the Great-West Life Assurance Co. for lining Osborne Street with two fantastic corporate structures, completed in 1958 and 1983, respectively. We hate the Great-West Life Assurance Co. for flattening two entire residential blocks to make way for the surface-parking lots you can not see behind these buildings. We're fickle that way.

The demolition of an Army Surplus store on Portage Avenue allowed the University of Winnipeg to continue its amoeba-like expansion across the western edge of downtown. The Buhler Centre encompasses both university space and the new home for the Plug In Institute of Contemporary Art.

If you get too close to the northern edge of the Winnipeg Art Gallery, it will cut you like a razor blade. That's how architects used to roll in 1970. Inside, however, there's a soft, creamy centre.

Downtown's Millennium Library illustrates the temporal anomaly known as Manitoba time, as it actually opened in 2004. Millennium Library Park, shown here, didn't open until 2012. Consider it 988 years early. It's better that way.

ABOVE / Until the Canadian Museum for Human Rights showed up, Esplanade Riel was Winnipeg's signature structure. Many of the pedestrian bridge's original critics shut the hell up after every bloody postcard for the city started featuring this thing, albeit from a distance, where you can't see the Sals' logo, since removed.

LEFT / Viewed here from the southeast, Manitoba Hydro's ultra-energy-efficient, 22-storey downtown headquarters features a solar chimney, geothermal heating and cooling, automatic windows, automated solar shading and toilets that transform human faeces into panda-bear food. That last claim may be spurious, but you do get a lot for $283 million.

57

ABOVE / Why just build new when you can also destroy old? The new terminal building at James Armstrong Richardson International Airport opened in 2011 as part of a $700-million makeover at what used to be simply known as Winnipeg International. Designed by César Pelli of Petronas Towers fame, the new terminal replaced a modernist structure considered an architectural triumph when it opened in 1964. The Winnipeg Airports Authority demolished the old structure in 2012, with tacit approval from Transport Canada.

RIGHT / Shown here with its face off in 2011, the $351-million Canadian Museum for Human Rights will be the first federal museum located outside Ottawa when it opens in 2014. There are hopes the Antoine Predock-designed structure will do for Winnipeg what the Frank Gehry-designed Guggenheim Museum did for Bilbao, Spain — make a relatively obscure city a destination for architectural tourism. The completed museum is topped by an illuminated Tower of Hope, a fitting pinnacle for a megaproject long destined to be a lightning rod for criticism.

4

AND YOU WILL KNOW US
BY THE TRAIL OF RUST ...

Spend any time in Winnipeg and you cannot fail but notice the complex relationship between the city and its residents. Winnipeggers tend to love their home with the fiery intensity of a thousand supernovae. They also tend to loathe the city like an all-too-familiar relative. Any public display of boosterism in Winnipeg typically provokes an equal and opposite expression of self-hatred, because to be a Winnipegger is to be conflicted about where you live and why you live there.

The reasons for this unsettled state of mind are legion. For starters, Winnipeg endures a highly variable climate that's among the most extreme in the world. There is an 81-degree divide between the city's highest recorded temperature (40.6° C on Aug. 7, 1949) and its lowest (-45° C on Feb. 18, 1966). The average July high is 26° C. The average January low is -23° C. It's not uncommon for the city to experience both a spring flood and drought-like summer conditions within the same calendar year. The only part of the planet to endure more variability than the Canadian prairies is the innermost interior of central Asia, where the Mongolian capital of Ulaan Bator has the dubious distinction of being even more bipolar than Winnipeg.

Winnipeg's climate is a byproduct of its location near the centre of North America. But this geographic placement also has psychological and cultural effects, as Winnipeg is isolated from just about everywhere else. The nearest city to Winnipeg to boast a larger population is Minneapolis-St. Paul, eight hours and 734 kilometres away by car.

The nearest Canadian centre with a larger population is Calgary, 13 hours and 1,327 kilometres to the west.

You could argue distance is irrelevant in an era when much of the planet's population interacts with each other online. But Winnipeg's lack of proximity to more cosmopolitan centres means its residents are less able to physically interact with people in other communities. As a result, they form more social connections within the city, which can feel like the world's largest small town. This phenomenon has positive benefits, as most Winnipeggers possess a very strong and powerful sense of identity. On the flipside, the city can feel claustrophobic to people born here and impenetrable to newcomers. Never mind six degrees of separation: In Winnipeg, two individuals usually can be connected in only two steps, if they don't have one person in common.

Along with the extreme climate and geographic isolation, Winnipeggers are also encumbered with a half-remembered sense of history. As children, most if not all of the city's

residents are imbued with at least a vague sense the city was once a very important centre, in the geopolitical context of North America as a whole. Winnipeg's century-long descent into ordinariness has given some of its residents a profound inferiority complex, as they compare the way the city is to the way it was and the way they want it to be.

In any of Winnipeg's older neighbourhoods, you will encounter spectacular remnants from Winnipeg's early industrial boom, when railways, factories and warehouses sprouted like iron, steel and stone weeds. Century-old buildings bear scars both modern and ancient, from last week's graffiti to the sixty-three-year-old high-water-mark from the 1950 Red River flood. A ridiculous abundance of vestigial rail lines bisect entire neighbourhoods, congest traffic and generate magically resonant sounds at all hours of the night. The faded remains of advertisements painted onto stone walls entice the ghosts of boomtown-era arrivals to purchase goods that no longer exist. And the underutilized lines of the Canadian Pacific Railway's massive Winnipeg Yards stretch out like the exposed skeletons of ancient serpents charged with dividing the North End from Winnipeg's south.

Arlington Bridge, which crosses the CPR Winnipeg Yards, provides crucial habitat for the rock dove, also known as the "flying rat" or "pigeon." It was completed in 1912 and dogged by bogus urban legends it was intended to cross the Nile River in Egypt, where pigeons have existed for at least 300,000 years.

Encountering all this unfulfilled promise can inspire a sense of Weltschmerz, the world-weary sadness that doesn't quite translate from German. And it's possible to derive a sort of beauty from this sadness, the way the photographs do throughout this chapter and this book.

Unfortunately, this disjunction between the Winnipeg That Exists and the Winnipeg That Was can manifest as an irrational sense of entitlement among a populace that feels it deserves to have a world-class stadium/museum/ water park/whatever. It may also lead Winnipeggers to seek some pathetic form of affirmation from visiting celebrities. Most onerously, some of the locals constantly strive for recognition from other centres. Psychologically, some Winnipeggers want to believe a city of 700,000 people is somehow more special than it is.

The truth is, people living in other parts of North America do not think much about Winnipeg, if they ever think about the city at all. If it weren't for the NHL's Jets and intermittent natural disasters, Winnipeg would never appear in international news reports. And the city's most famous cultural exports don't exactly paint a postcard-perfect picture of the place.

Over the course of a fifty-year recording career, what Neil Young recalls in song about his four-year stint in Winnipeg in the 1960s are "the punches came fast and hard" in the schoolyard after he arrived from Toronto and how the corner of Portage & Main felt like "50 below." One Great City, arguably the most popular song by The Weakerthans, invites audiences to sing along with the "I hate Winnipeg" chorus. Filmmaker Guy Maddin's love-and-hate letter to the city, My Winnipeg, portrays its residents as existing in an eternal state of icy, suspended animation. The narration at the beginning of the mockumentary exemplifies a profound state of ambivalence:

Winnipeg, Winnipeg, Winnipeg.
Snowy, sleepwalking Winnipeg.
My home for my entire life.
My entire life.
I must leave it.
I must leave it.
I must leave it now.

Of course, none of these artists actually shaped the reputation Winnipeg does in fact enjoy in other Canadian centres. Outside of hipster-intelligentsia circles (Where you may travel! You're reading a book, for God's sake!), real people don't pay too much attention to cultural producers. They pay attention to the anonymous guy on Yahoo Answers who says "Winnipeg is the biggest shithole in the country" when faced with a well-meaning question about tourist attractions in the city.

When people in other Canadian cities do in fact think about Winnipeg, this is the predominant sentiment, along with vague notions about snow, mosquitoes, floods, high homicide rates and irrationally loyal sports fans. And historically speaking, there is a semblance of truth to back up the idea that Winnipeg really is a shithole.

Before the 1910 completion of the St. Andrews Lock and Dam, which moderates the flow of the Red River north of Winnipeg, seasonal variations in river levels could reduce the city's largest waterway to a little ribbon. This was no big deal before the city existed. But when the residents of what was at first Fort Garry and later Winnipeg started spilling human waste into the city's rivers, both the Red and the Assiniboine started to smell like sewers, especially during the fall.

The poor state of sanitation in Winnipeg during its early years was compounded by the fact many residents initially drew their water from the very same rivers. High rates of typhoid fever, a bowel disorder caused by a salmonella variant, were blamed on the absence of both a modern sewage system and adequate drinking-water supplies around the turn of the last century. Many of the typhoid victims were poor eastern European immigrants who lived in the North End.

Initially, the sad state of the city's rivers did not bother the city's affluent, English-speaking elite, who tended to have access to safe water from artesian wells. But that changed in 1904, when a fire at hardware magnate James Ashdown's Main Street store led fire officials to flood a well-water distribution system with the fetid gumbo from the Red River. Hundreds of affluent folks contracted typhoid, sparking the political will to seek out a safe, new water source for the City of Winnipeg. That turned out to be Indian Bay on Shoal Lake, which was connected to the city in 1919 by a 155-kilometre-long, gravity-powered aqueduct.

By the time the aqueduct was completed, infectious disease rates in Winnipeg were among the worst in North America. The 1919 General Strike further tarred the city's reputation across North America, with the New York Times reporting the rise of Bolshevism in the city.

As a result, Winnipeg became a stinking, fetid Communist hellhole in the popular imagination of Canadians going into the 1920s. This was manna for Torontonians in particular, who already had a reason to hate the Manitoba capital.

Fifteen years earlier, 1905 Winnipeg was Canada's third-largest city, behind only Toronto and then-dominant Montreal. At the time, Winnipeg had yet to become the butt of winter and mosquito jokes. It was a fast-growing prairie metropolis whose economic alliance with the port city of Montreal actually threatened business interests on the shores of Lake Ontario. Toronto, which had a trade alliance of its own with Vancouver, had a legitimate economic reason to disparage the Chicago of the North.

While this rivalry has faded away, a vestige remains in the form of Toronto's irrational and continuing disdain for anything connected to Winnipeg. Torontonians no longer know why they hate Winnipeg, but the mere mention of the city can inspire expressions of pity and disgust. And when this wave of derision collides with Winnipeg's own inferiority complex, the resulting disturbance creates a cascade of negative harmonic waves that cancel each other out.

Winnipeggers feel like they own the right to hate their own city. But if someone else hates it, too — look out. Hell hath no fury like a Winnipegger insulted. We do a fine job of doing it ourselves.

Ultimately, all the warehouse monoliths and railway tentacles that persevere from the industrial boom add up to a monument worthy of Shelley's Ozymandias: "My name is Winnipeg, city of cities. Look upon my works, ye mighty, and despair."

No problem, big guy. Despair is what we do best. ◼

Starting in 1881, Montreal's Ogilvie Flour Mills built a sprawling complex in South Point Douglas. The Five Roses brand — which originated in Kenora, Ont. — was brought under the Ogilvie umbrella in 1954. All but abandoned by 1989, the complex was burned by arsonists and most of it was eventually demolished by the city in 2005. The surviving warehouse portion stands watch over Higgins Avenue.

Built in 1911, the Louise Bridge will be replaced in the coming decade and
may be converted into a bike-and-pedestrian crossing. An 1881 bridge at
the same site carried the first rail cars across the Red River, allowing the
Canadian Pacific Railway to set up shop in Winnipeg instead of Selkirk,
50 kilometres to the north. Selkirk, it must be noted, tends to flood a lot often.

Up until 1906, Winnipeg drew most its water from artesian wells, which provided safe drinking water for the relatively wealthy elite but were not particularly useful for fighting fires. The construction of the James Avenue High Pressure Pumping Station was spearheaded by hardware magnate James Ashdown, whose Main Street store caught fire in 1904 — and was only saved by pumping silty Red River water into the city's drinking-water supply. The move resulted in more than 1,000 cases of typhoid, allowing affluent Winnipeggers to share something in common with immigrants living in the North End, who often got sick from drinking water straight out of the Red. The pumping station was hooked up to the Winnipeg Aqueduct in 1919 and operated until 1986. Its fate remains uncertain, even though it still houses massive gears and other vintage machinery that practically define the steampunk esthetic.

"Blue skies! Nothing but blue skies!" The ass end of The Yellow Warehouse, on Main Street.

Chambers Street is made up of two blocks of not much in particular on either side of Logan Avenue. You've never been there, yet you somehow feel you have.

Dominion Bridge used to fabricate steel at this sprawling Dublin Avenue site, which still houses heavy industry but also been used as a movie set. Guy Maddin, Winnipeg's most well-known filmmaker, shot Twilight Of The Ice Nymphs inside the main building. In the foreground sits Omand's Creek, which despite its ditch-like appearance is one of Winnipeg eight official waterways. The middle section of the creek is artificial; It was dug to divert the waters of Colony Creek into the Assiniboine River much further west of its original outflow, near the present site of the Granite Curling Club.

FAR LEFT / The J.R. Watkins Company Warehouse, erected on Annabella Street in 1914, served a company that originally described itself as a manufacturer of "spices & toilet articles, extracts and proprietary medicines." The warehouse is now home to Richlu, one of Winnipeg's last surviving garment manufacturers. They make parkas, which is the closest thing to a divine mission as there is in this town.

LEFT / Central Grain sits so close to Archibald Street, there's barely room for a sidewalk. The company manufactures feed for cattle, bison, horses and elk, in case you ever wondered whether you can buy a box of Wapiti Chow along with a can of Whiskas.

Irony, thy name is Winnipeg Cold Storage Company. Average January high: -13C. Average January low: -23 C.

The CPR Mainline slices through Point Douglas, separating a revitalizing residential neighbourhood from a fading industrial area that may very well become prime condospace.

*RIGHT / More often than not,
Winnipeg's homicide rate allows
the city to claim the dubious title
of Canada's murder capital.
And as it happens, motorists
driving along Springfield Road
are offered one hell of a deal.*

*BELOW / clockwise from left:
The CPR Winnipeg Yards, the
Red River, downtown, the Health
Sciences Centre complex and
at bottom right, the National
Microbiology Laboratory, where
the anthrax and ebola live.*

*FAR RIGHT / Time stands still on
the Red River: The CN Rail
Bridge, with Vieux Saint-Boniface
at left and Esplanade Riel in
the distance.*

5 ARTERIES AND VEINS

In France, all citizens are entitled to "liberty, equality and fraternity." In the US, it's "life, liberty and the pursuit of happiness." Canada strives for "peace, order and good government," Cuba pledges "homeland or death" and little Luxembourg modestly declares "we wish to remain what we are." Aim high, Luxembourg!

Winnipeg's official motto is "one with the strength of many," a reference to city's amalgamation with thirteen of its former suburbs in 1972. But every Winnipegger knows this isn't a mission statement.

At the core of a Winnipegger's belief system is the notion of a God-given freedom to drive wherever they want and park wherever they want — ideally right in front of wherever it is they're going — with no charges or time limitations or any other rules upsetting the inviolable sanctity of their automobile's right to pointlessly take up space.

Winnipeg is an automobile city, but not like Detroit or Oshawa, where they actually make the damn things. Winnipeggers love to drive because the size, scale and layout of the city forces them to do so. Beginning at a very early age, when young Winnipeggers learn about the inconveniences and indignities of public transit, they yearn to own and operate their own shiny little box of

carbon-dioxide-spewing metal that will forever consign themselves to a future of road rage, debt and obsessive gasoline-price watching.

You could argue this makes Winnipeggers no different from anyone else in North America, or at least residents of sprawling, pedestrian-unfriendly cities such as Phoenix or Los Angeles. But the combination of climate, layout and history makes Winnipeg a bizarre entry in the list of the world's most automobile-reliant places.

Winnipeg's love affair with the car goes back to an early reliance on the ox-cart, a mode of transportation during the settlement area. In the 1800s, Red River Valley settlers required the strength of oxen to haul their goods across dirt tracks that were muddy in the summer, covered in snow in the winter and dusty the rest of the time. As a result, some of Winnipeg's first major arteries — Main Street and Portage Avenue in particular — were built wide enough

The four sentinels of Portage & Main — The Richardson Building, the Bank of Montreal tower, the Commodity Exchange Tower and 201 Portage Ave. — stand watch over Winnipeg's best-known intersection.

Approaching Portage & Main, everything is illuminated.

Downtown's Notre Dame Avenue, not to be confused with Rue Notre Dame across the river in St. Boniface. Sometimes it sucks to drive a cab or deliver pizzas in Winnipeg.

to allow ox-carts to pass each other. A century later, the width of the streets would make it really easy to move motor vehicles through downtown instead of around the city's core.

Initially, Winnipeg's layout followed the French-Canadian custom of carving out long, narrow river lots. Farms belonging to both Francophone, Catholic Métis and Anglophone, Protestant settlers were typically long, shallow rectangles of land that extend back from the Red and Assiniboine Rivers. Just like on the St. Lawrence River in Quebec, many of these lots grew narrower with each generation, as families subdivided properties for their children.

This pattern of elongated blocks remains visible in the city's older residential areas. In the Kildonans, Elmwood and St. Vital, blocks along the avenues extending east and west from the Red River are longer than the north-south streets. Conversely, in the West End, River Heights and St. James, the north-south blocks on streets emanating from the Assiniboine River are longer than the east-west streets.

As residents poured into Winnipeg in the late 1800s, the long blocks were subdivided into grids, as was the Anglo-Canadian custom. But these grids didn't match up to each other as they grew together, partly because each was oriented to its own stretch of a meandering Red or Assiniboine — and also because there were a lot more waterways to contend with.

Today, Winnipeg has eight official waterways — four rivers and four creeks, all considered navigable until Ottawa redefined that concept in 2012. In reality, only the Red, Assiniboine and La Salle rivers can support watercraft of some sort during the entire ice-free season. The Seine River, which wanders through St. Vital and St. Boniface, can be paddled by canoe during the spring, as can

sections of Sturgeon Creek in St. James and the more central Omand's Creek for a very brief window following the snowmelt. Truro Creek in St. James and Bunn's Creek in North Kildonan are not navigable by any means other than snowshoe.

In the 1870s, there were several more creeks confounding early Winnipeg developers, along with wetlands and at least one sizable oxbow lake. Just like in Holland, where the demand for land led to massive drainage and diking projects along the North Sea, Winnipeg drained as many bodies of water as it could to create room for more homes on more streets.

In Norwood and Old St. Boniface, Enfield Crescent follows the edge of an old oxbow lake that once straddled the two neighbourhoods. In the North End, a creek once ran alongside Pritchard Avenue to the Red River. And until 1895, a body of water variously known as Sinclair's Creek, Brown's Creek and Ross's Creek ran through what's now Red River College's downtown campus, across the edge of city hall and then down along William and Bannatyne Avenue to the Red River. The Royal Manitoba Theatre Centre now stands in its place.

Most significantly, the city filled in almost the entire length of Colony Creek, which originally emptied into the Assiniboine River west of the Manitoba Legislature. Colony Creek was diverted through an artificial channel to Omand's Creek, which continues to face development pressure from Polo Park commercial land owners.

By the time the creeks were out of the way, rail lines presented new obstacles for connecting city neighbourhoods. But the massive pace of Winnipeg's turn-of-the-century growth gave city administrators no option but to keep on building regardless of connectivity. The combined result of the rail lines, waterways, both the French and English grid system and pre-settlement footpaths left Winnipeg with all sorts of quirks, some of them beloved by its residents and others that simply serve as annoyances.

For example, Notre Dame Avenue was forced to run from the northwest to the southeast in a compromise effort to match up the off-kilter angles of an Assiniboine-spawned Upper Fort Garry/West End street grid with a Red River-generated downtown/North End grid. This created triangular lots with marvelous buildings such as the Breadalbane Block, which rose at the corner of Cumberland Avenue and Hargrave Street in 1909.

The Corydon-Pembina Interchange, a five-street confluence better known as Confusion Corner, was an attempt to extend a new regional street across an old river trail without getting tangled up in the Fort Rouge railyards.

And as neighbourhoods grew into each other, roads were combined and sometimes realigned to form city-wide routes that were granted numerical designations to avoid the confusion posed by multiple street names. Route 62, for example, starts on Salter Street in West Kildonan before morphing into Isabel Street, Balmoral Street, Colony Street, Memorial Boulevard, Osborne Street, Dunkirk Street and finally Dakota Street before it ends in South St. Vital.

In older neighbourhoods, the quirkiness of Winnipeg's roads remains as a testament to the city's railway, settlement and First Nations history. But after the Second World War, the city succumbed to the same homogenizing influences that reduced vast areas of other North American centres into look-alike Edge Cities, each one as indistinguishable from the other as mass-produced brands of beer.

The creation of postwar suburbs with front driveways instead of back lanes spelled the end of building new neighbourhoods along a network of grid roads. It also meant new homes wouldn't have front porches and that front yards would serve only ornamental purposes. This was done to ease the use of the passenger vehicle, the symbol of postwar prosperity, but had the secondary effect of isolating neighbours from each other. Many of the new developments also had cul-de-sacs and winding streets that were intended to discourage through-traffic, but the maze-like developments came with another unintended consequence — people stopped walking because they couldn't get anywhere quickly on foot.

As more people drove or rode in cars, public transit became less important. Winnipeg's electric streetcar system, which dated back to 1892, was dismantled in the 1960s and replaced with diesel buses. Transportation planners called for the construction of a subway, but the city spent the next fifty years expanding regional roads instead.

A bus corridor that would have formed the start of a rapid-transit system was recommended in the 1970s. The city completed the first 3.6 kilometres in 2012, thirty-six years and six mayors later.

What's now a large and sprawling city, relative to its population, has saddled taxpayers with too much in the way of road, water and sewer infrastructure, all of it expensive to maintain. For financial and environmental reasons, Winnipeg has no choice but to increase its population density. But the mistakes of the postwar period are not easily undone. Neither are attitudes about cars, despite a recent upswing in transit ridership and bicycle commuting.

The creation of new bike paths in 2010 sparked a noisy but short-lived backlash from motorists. The prospect of spending hundreds of millions more on bus corridors angers drivers who would rather see the city repave the potholes created by Winnipeg's never-ending freeze-thaw cycles.

But Winnipeg's healthiest, most vibrant neighbourhoods remain the ones where people walk and actually enjoy being on the street.

The promise of amalgamation — "one with the strength of many" — was that the city's suburbs would no longer detrimentally affect its older neighbourhoods. This will only be a promise as long as Winnipeggers continue to love their cars more than they love themselves. ■

Main Street, looking slick again. The sign in the cabaret window may be the least suggestive image in the frame.

A look at pedestrian-friendly Albert Street, prior to the destruction of the Albert Street Business Block, the low-slung structure in the middle. The block, which included a portion of one of Winnipeg's oldest homes, was severely damaged in a 2012 electrical fire and subsequently demolished.

RIGHT & ABOVE / McDermot Avenue exemplifies the timelessness of the Exchange District. The snowy stretch lies west of Main Street; the rainy stretch is the on east side.

FAR RIGHT / Anyone can tell the time by the angle of shadows. Winnipeggers can estimate the temperature by the thickness of the steam rising from manholes. This one lies on Hargrave Street.

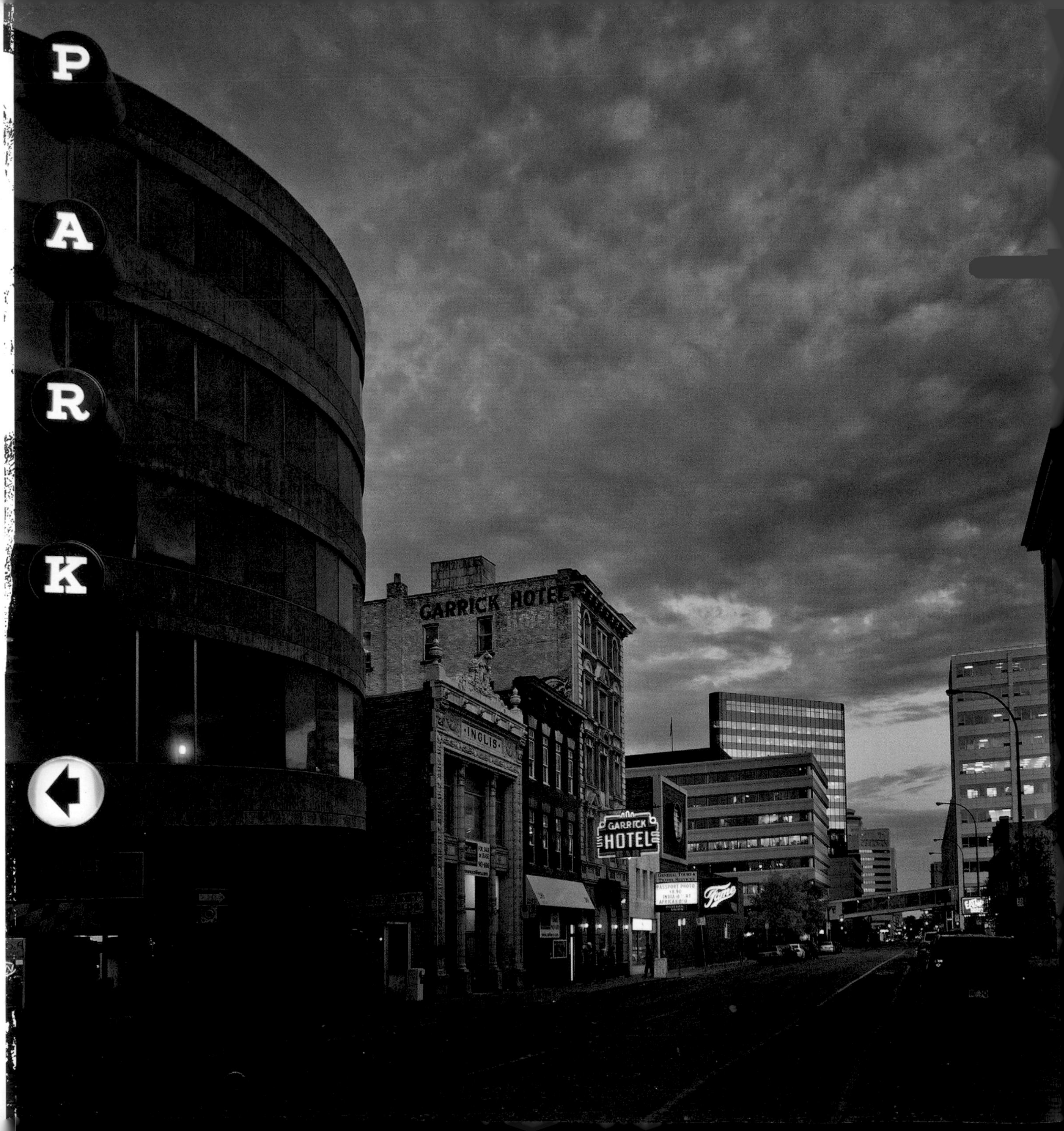
P
A
R
K
GARRICK HOTEL
INGLIS
GARRICK
HOTEL
Fame

RIGHT / Graham Avenue, also known as Graham Mall, a corridor for Winnipeg Transit buses. The plan is for transit to hasten development. Any day now, anyway.

BELOW / When and if the sun finally sets on the Hudson's Bay Company Winnipeg flagship store, the folks who dwell within the Manitoba Legislature will be asked to come up with a rescue plan. The health of downtown's northwestern corner depends on some from of tenant remaining in The Bay.

LEFT / Garry Street is an architectural jumble. The circular parkade in the left foreground wraps around a main-floor restaurant space. The skywalk at right leads into the former Canada Post complex, which now serves as headquarters for the Winnipeg Police Service.

ABOVE / A southwestern view of Crescentwood from Wellington Crescent, with Cockburn Street gleaming at left and Dorchester Avenue trailing off at right.

RIGHT / Until its reconstruction in 1992, you couldn't see out the sides of Arlington Bridge from a vantage point inside a passenger vehicle. Now the full glory of the CPR Winnipeg Yards comes into view.

LEFT / It took 36 years, six mayors and $138 million to build the first 3.6 kilometres of the Southwest Transitway, Winnipeg's first rapid-transit corridor. The price tag also covered Osborne Station, whose stylishness exceeded expectations.

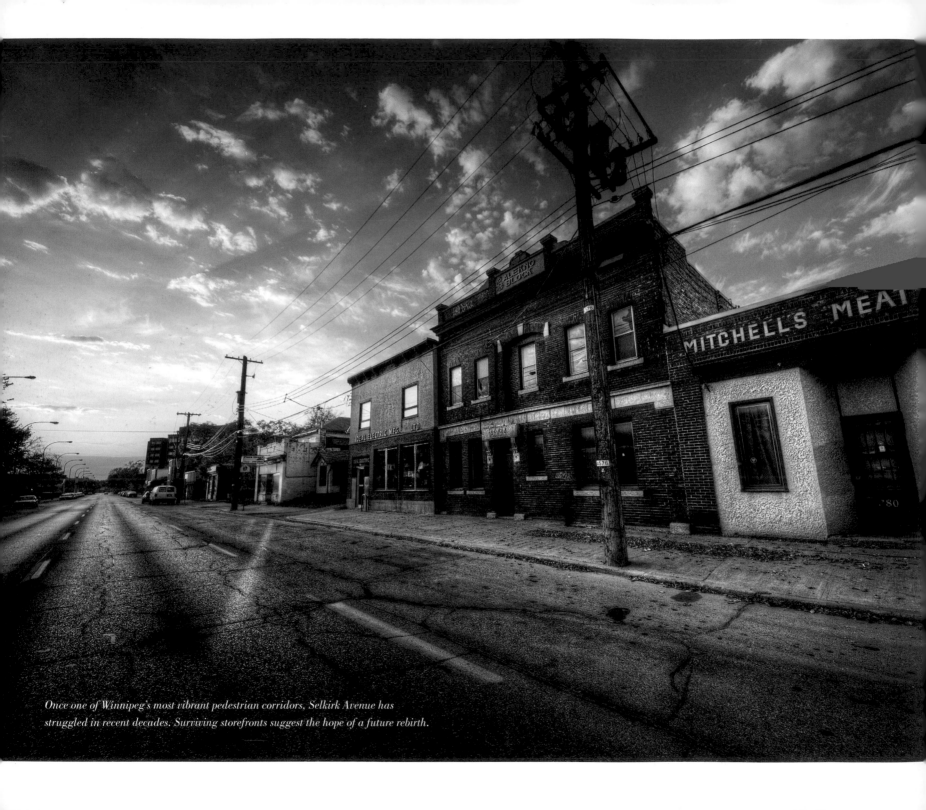

*Once one of Winnipeg's most vibrant pedestrian corridors, Selkirk Avenue has
struggled in recent decades. Surviving storefronts suggest the hope of a future rebirth.*

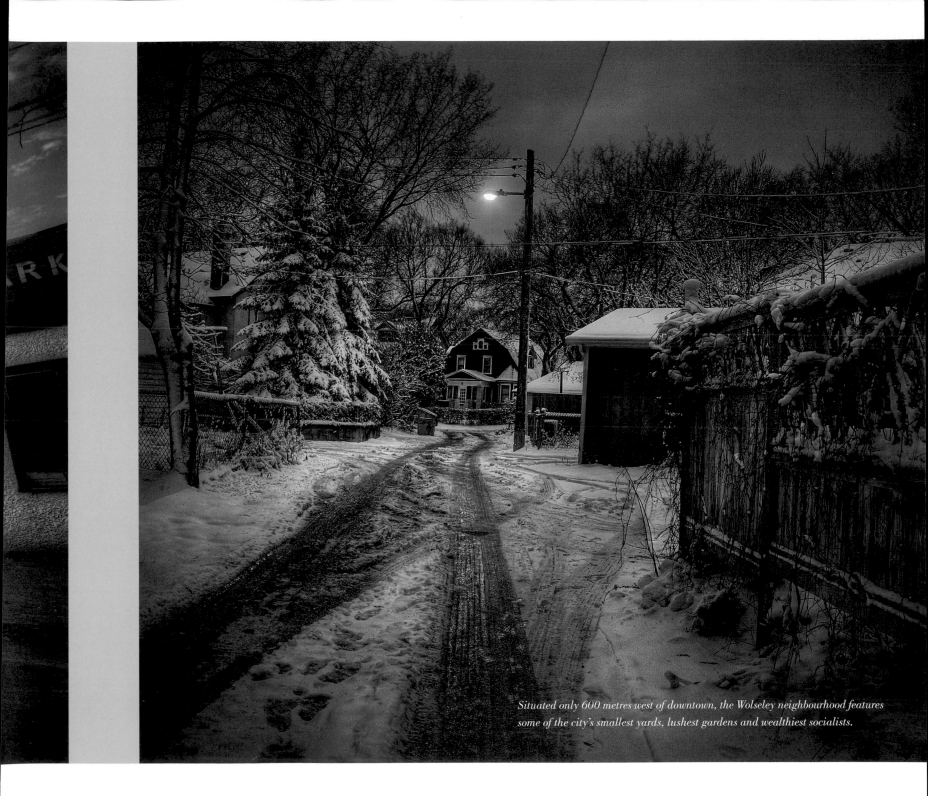

Situated only 600 metres west of downtown, the Wolseley neighbourhood features some of the city's smallest yards, lushest gardens and wealthiest socialists.

ABOVE / Winnipeg is made of money, as you'll find at the corner of Sherbrook Street and Portage Avenue.

RIGHT / Lightning strikes through the leading edge of a thunderstorm hovering over Main Street. From upper left to bottom right: Towering cumulonimbus, shelf-like arcus and wispy fractus clouds.

92

6 BAD DECISIONS

In 1883, the year after the railway arrived in Winnipeg, the fast-growing young city was in desperate need of better infrastructure. Faced with a desire to straighten out Main Street, demolition crews went to work tearing down the east wall of Upper Fort Garry, the birthplace of both the City of Winnipeg and the Province of Manitoba.

By 1888, every structure on the old fort's grounds, except for a single gate, was dismantled for reuse as building supplies or firewood. The eradication of Upper Fort Garry marked the beginning of a proud Winnipeg tradition: reducing heritage structures to rubble without really considering the consequences.

Over the next 120 years, the footprint of the old fort went on to house a lacrosse club, a stadium, Imperial Oil's regional headquarters, Metro Winnipeg's pre-amalgamation offices and a City of Winnipeg public works building. Finally, a volunteer group called The Friends of Upper Fort Garry acquired the site and reduced it to rubble once again, save for the gate that escaped the original demolition. A heritage park is planned for some time in the future. But as this book goes to print, Winnipeg's birthplace remains a weed lot.

When history repeats itself, it's supposed to be tragedy the first time and farce on the second go-round.

Karl Marx didn't include a road map for a third repeat occurrence. That's too bad, given how Winnipeg has stumbled along for 140 years, committing and recommitting the same crimes against the cause of not just heritage conservation, but transportation planning, economic development, inner-city renewal and... well, just about any municipal enterprise that requires careful consideration.

Now before you consider this assessment unfair, it must be noted Winnipeg has done a lot of things right over the years. The 1919 construction of the Winnipeg Aqueduct, an engineering marvel that continues to meet all the city's drinking-water needs, was a forward-thinking work of genius. The 1972 amalgamation of the city with its suburbs was thirty years ahead of the municipal-governance curve in Canada. And few cities on earth do as good a job of fighting repeated floods, cleaning up after blizzards and killing mosquito larvae by the billions. Of course, it's quite probable no other city has to engage in all three of those tasks on a regular basis.

62 NORTH
Osborne St

95 WEST
Corydon Ave

42 NORTH
Donald St

42 SOUTH
Pembina Hwy

MULVEY

James Allum

While some cities build overpasses, Winnipeg likes to keep things simple.

But there is a sense of déjà vu attached to the decision-making at city hall. And this goes far beyond the repeatedly unlearned lesson that when you allow historically important structures to fall into disrepair, they must be torn down.

Urban-revitalization efforts appear particularly Sisyphean, as generations of politicians and planners have fallen in love with the idea one big project can cure all that ails downtown.

The problem with Winnipeg's core is the absence of density, which is really just an absence of people. Downtown, which began its existence on Main Street before expanding to the west along Portage Avenue, is too big for a city the size of Winnipeg and has too few people living within its bounds. But only recently have the city and province come to accept the idea that the best way to bring more people to the area is to create policies that encourage the construction of more apartments and condominiums. And not coincidentally, only recently has downtown started to achieve a modest semblance of renewal.

For the preceding fifty years, however, the megaproject was the renewal vehicle of choice. The first of the downtown-revitalization megaprojects was the creation of the Civic Centre campus, an ensemble of concrete and Tyndall-stone modernist buildings completed in 1964. What used to be four square blocks west of Main Street were razed to make way for Winnipeg's new city hall, a Public Safety Building to serve as police headquarters, three concrete plazas and the Civic Centre Parkade. The parkade was shuttered due to structural concerns in 2012, while the skyrocketing price of recladding the Public Safety Building led the police to move into a new home

south of Graham Avenue. Only city hall survived the first half-century of renewal.

A handful of years later, from 1968 to 1970, the province set to work extending the modernist ensemble on the east side of Main Street. To celebrate Manitoba's first century, more blocks were razed to make way for the Centennial Concert Hall, the Manitoba Museum, the Royal Manitoba Theatre Centre and yet more concrete plazas. The $100-million project was intended to revitalize the east side of the Exchange. Instead, the mass of concrete stuck out like an island of emotionally distant modernism amid an increasingly empty landscape east of Main Street.

Next up, in the 1970s, the entire block at the southwest corner of Portage and Main was taken out to make room for the Commodity Exchange Tower and the subterranean Winnipeg Square, both of which connected to the city's new weather-protected walkway system, a series of tunnels and skywalks that prevent pedestrians from coming into contact with the outside world. Most heinously, barricades were erected at Portage and Main to prevent pedestrians from crossing Canada's most famous intersection. This effectively ensured the men and women of Winnipeg's financial district never had to expose their skin to sunlight again, unless they wanted to buy a hotdog or have a cigarette. The barricades will remain up until 2017 at the earliest.

The 1980s brought the mother of all downtown Winnipeg megaprojects: The redevelopment of the north side of Portage Avenue. Six more city blocks were expropriated and flattened to make room for the mall known as Portage Place, a new YM-YWCA and several apartment towers. A $71-million government contribution leveraged another $300-million worth of private investment in the colossus, which allowed the weather-protected

Portage & Main, Winnipeg's most famous intersection,
can not be crossed on foot, thanks to the 1979 deal to build
the Commodity Exchange Tower and Winnipeg Square,
an underground mall that serves as a key link in the city's
weather-protected walkway system. Tourists still make a sport
of jumping the barricades, which will remain until 2017,
when the agreement expires. The ones who do venture
underground in an effort to cross the street legally can get
lost in the catacombs, where they are forced to survive on
 a meagre diet of Starbucks coffee and takeout sushi.
Welcome to Winnipeg, folks. Now do not leave the mall.
You may discover a city out there.

97

Manitoba's stately Law Courts building, erected in 1916, is violated by a skywalk extending across Vaughan Street. The assault has so far gone unpunished.

walkway system to extend from Portage and Main to The Bay. But within weeks of Portage Place's 1987 opening, stores on the south side of Portage Avenue complained of the absence of foot traffic. By the mid-1990s, empty storefronts on the eastern stretch of Portage Avenue stood as a testament to the mall's inability to serve as a catalyst for more development — and the decline of the retail sector in all but the largest of North America's historic downtowns.

Hot on the heels of Portage Place, all three levels of government and private investors sunk a combined $76 million into an effort to decommission the desolate railyards at the confluence of the Red and Assiniboine Rivers and transform the historic area into a waterfront tourist attraction. The Forks was hailed as an immediate success when its first amenities — an indoor market, a river port and national historic site — opened in 1989. Over the next two decades, most of the newly reclaimed green space was swallowed up by the addition of an outdoor stage, a children's museum and theatre, a parkade, a hotel, a skate park and finally the Canadian Museum for Human Rights, a $351-million megaproject in its own right. Despite its popularity, The Forks remains disconnected from the rest of downtown and still has yet to become financially self-sufficient: revenues from Portage Place's underground parkade keep what's now The Forks-North Portage Partnership afloat.

To the north of The Forks, at the turn of the millennium, all three levels of government poured another $30-million into the construction of a riverfront baseball diamond now known as Shaw Park, the Esplanade Riel pedestrian bridge and the creation of Waterfont Drive, home to a series of new condos that were quickly sold but not immediately occupied. The latter project was supposed to inject more people into the city's core, but the development's location at downtown's eastern fringe meant the new residents were all but invisible. It would take another decade before the area would achieve some sort of critical mass.

Not content to stop there, the public and private sector teamed up to spend another $134 million on MTS Centre, a downtown hockey arena built on the site of the former Eaton's Building, which wasn't quite large enough for the project but wound up getting demolished anyway. The 15,000-seat venue opened in 2004 and did little to spark further development until 2011, when the return of the Winnipeg Jets emboldened the city to embark on — wait for it — another megaproject. The latest scheme: Convert eleven blocks at the centre of downtown into a sports, hospitality and entertainment district, where new property taxes can be plowed right back into area improvements.

Add in the $200-million expansion of the Winnipeg Convention Centre and elected officials have easily sunk more than $1 billion worth of public funds into downtown-revitalization efforts in a matter of decades. At some point, the private sector must step up and shoulder the rest of the burden.

If not, taxpayers will keep funding an endless cycle of expropriations, demolitions and construction, all in the name of saving downtown from the effects of the last effort to save downtown... and so on and so on. ◼

In the 1980s, the city flattened entire downtown blocks on the north side of Portage Avenue to make way for the North Portage development, which included Portage Place mall, completed in 1987. Initial hopes the mall would serve as a catalyst for downtown revitalization faded by the middle of the 1990s, as storefronts further east on Portage Avenue went dark. A 1998 external makeover improved the streetscape of the three-block-long monolith, which nonetheless stands as a monument to the futility of the megaproject approach to inner-city revitalization.

LEFT / Garish, neo-classical flourishes in Fort Garry Place make the mixed-use structure look like somebody with too much perfume smells: cheap. The tower portion also hovers over the Fort Garry Hotel like a creepy aunt or uncle who will not keep their distance. That said, when this thing was completed in 1989, it took another two decades for another downtown residential tower to even get started.

BELOW / The deal to create MTS Centre required the construction of a 15,000-seat hockey arena on the old Eaton's building footprint, which wasn't large enough for the job. So Hargrave Street was narrowed into a two-lane track that feels like a tunnel and effectively traps vehicles inside the parkade across the street from the arena following NHL games.

Winnipeg's birthplace, Upper Fort Garry, is a vacant surface lot awaiting conversion into a heritage monument. In 2008, a volunteer group called The Friends of Upper Fort Garry convinced the city to rescind a decision to allow an apartment tower to rise on the southwest corner of the site. A vacant city public works building that fronted on to Main Street was then torn down to make way for a heritage park and interpretive centre, neither of which existed as of 2013.

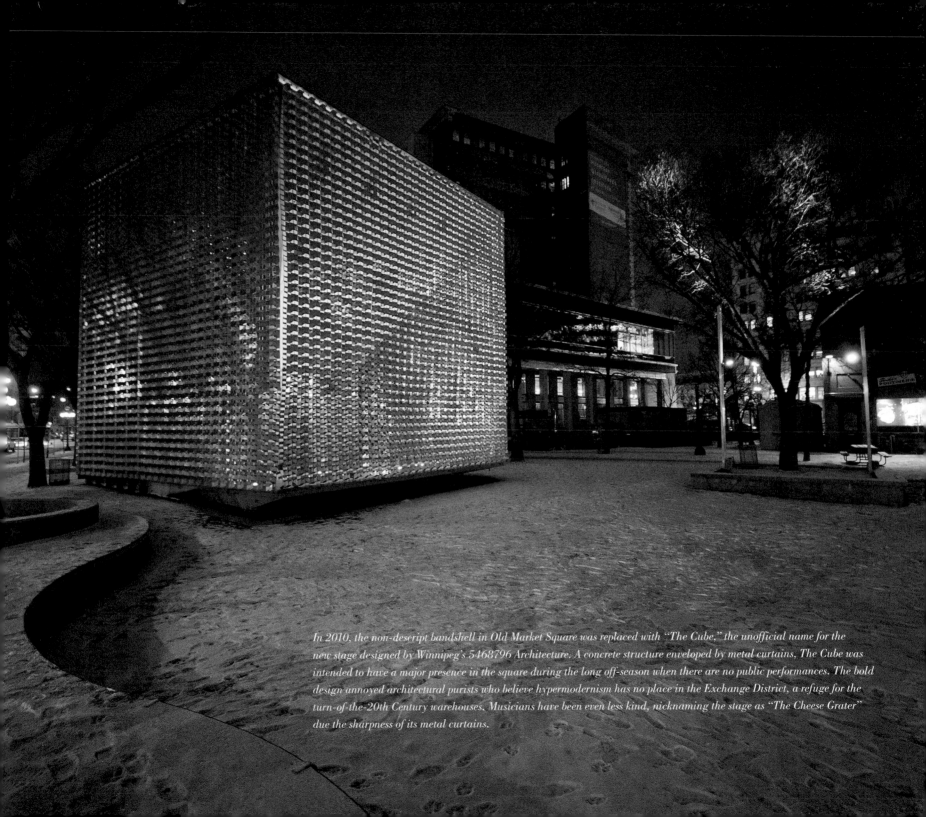

In 2010, the non-descript bandshell in Old Market Square was replaced with "The Cube," the unofficial name for the new stage designed by Winnipeg's 5468796 Architecture. A concrete structure enveloped by metal curtains, The Cube was intended to have a major presence in the square during the long off-season when there are no public performances. The bold design annoyed architectural purists who believe hypermodernism has no place in the Exchange District, a refuge for the turn-of-the-20th Century warehouses. Musicians have been even less kind, nicknaming the stage as "The Cheese Grater" due the sharpness of its metal curtains.

RIGHT / In 1992 and 2004, the owner of the
Ryan Block asked the city for permission to
demolish the six-storey heritage building,
which had stood at the southwest corner
King Street and Bannatyne Avenue since 1895.
The city refused both times but allowed it to
fall in 2009 due to concerns about structural
integrity. To maintain the facades, a deal was
struck to build a parkade that would reconstruct
the Ryan Block's north and east-facing walls.
The resulting parkade is quite pleasant, as
far as parkades go, but nonetheless proves
property owners can in fact get away with
demolishing heritage buildings by simply
neglecting them.

BELOW / The brutalist Public Safety Building,
home to the Winnipeg Police Service until
2014, is part of a modernist ensemble of
civic structures. In 2006, the city set aside
$17 million to fix the PSB's crumbling
Tyndall-stone cladding. By 2012, that
mushroomed into a $194-million plan to
convert another downtown structure into a
new police headquarters. The future use of
the PSB is unknown, as the city may not be
able to sell the 1965 structure, thanks to a
public-use caveat placed on the land by the
original donor back in 1875.

104

The vacant patch of city-owned land known as Parcel Four is Winnipeg's most infamous surface-parking lot, having served at the centre of not one but two scandals at city hall. In 2008, city council narrowly approved a plan to retroactively amend a lease of the lot by Riverside Park Management, a non-profit organization that sublet the land to the Winnipeg Goldeyes, a business owned by the mayor at the time. Then in 2012, city officials unveiled a plan to build a water park at the site, directly opposite Waterfront Drive from the Canadian Museum of Human Rights. In the face of public outrage, city council allowed the idea to die.

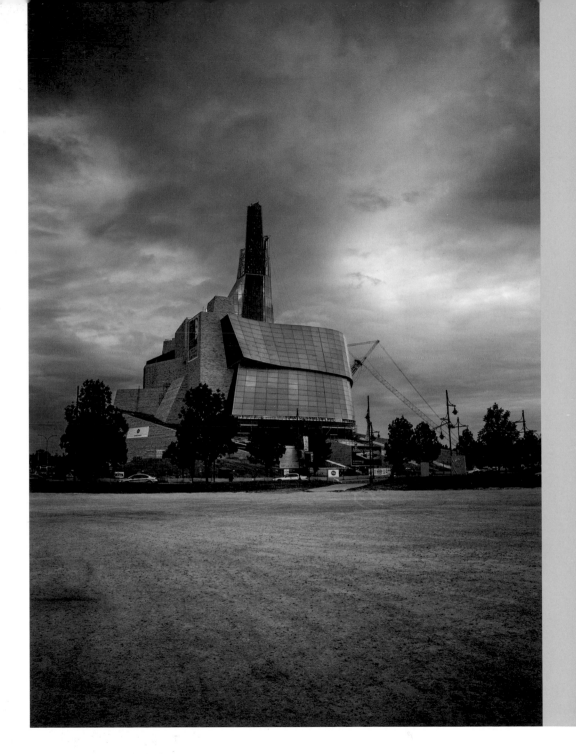

THINGS THAT SURVIVED DESPITE OUR BEST EFFORTS **TO DESTROY THEM**

7

In 1997, around the time Winnipeg was feeling as bad about itself as it ever would, Ottawa declared the Exchange District a national historic site.

Officially, this move was made to recognize the role played by Winnipeg's original commercial and financial district in opening up western Canada and developing the nation's economy at the turn of the twentieth century. While that may seem like a highly conceptual basis for a national historic site, there was also something physical to recognize: many of the structures from the city's original boom continue to stand within the twenty-one-block boundary of the Exchange District neighbourhood. A century after the end of Winnipeg's brief moment in the economic spotlight, the Exchange still possesses cut-stone and terra cotta warehouse buildings from the late nineteenth century as well as larger Chicago School structures such as the Confederation Life Building and Union Bank Tower, which face each other on Main Street.

It would be lovely to believe the survival of these buildings is the result of a deliberate effort to conserve

what policy geeks call "built heritage." It's also tempting to credit the city for developing rules and regulations governing the protection of structures deemed to be historically or architecturally unique. But the reality is a big reason the Exchange District still boasts century-old buildings, arch-covered back alleys and quaintly narrow streets is Winnipeg grew so slowly over most of the twentieth century, nobody had a chance to knock the damn things down.

With the notable exception of Montreal, every major city in Canada grew at a faster rate than Winnipeg after the end of the First World War. In 1911, at the height of Winnipeg's initial grandeur, the city ranked No. 3 among Canadian cities by population. That was a remarkable feat for a prairie settlement that only boasted a few hundred souls forty years earlier. But the rapid growth experienced during the railway boom would never be experienced again.

Some time during the 1920s, Vancouver overtook

The Royal Albert Arms was among Winnipeg's more upscale hotels when it opened in 1913 on Albert Street within a whisper of Portage & Main. As the Exchange District's fortunes waxed and waned, the Albert somehow managed to avoid demolition and Albert Street itself held on to its pedestrian-friendly streetscape. By the 1980s, the hotel was functioning as a low-end apartment building when punk rock and indie bands adopted the venue on the main floor as their unofficial home. Minneapolis' legendary Hüsker Dü recorded a cover of Eight Miles Here in the '80s and a then-little-known version of Green Day performed in the '90s. The venue went dark in 2011 due to the new owner's inability to afford repairs, and unfortunately remained closed as this book went to print.

Winnipeg to become Canada's third-largest city. By the 1931 census, there were 22,000 more people living in the BC city, which replaced the Manitoba capital as the most important economic centre in western Canada. The driving force behind Vancouver's growth was the grain-export business.

Metro Winnipeg had 284,000 people in 1931. It would take more than four decades for that figure to double. During that same timeframe, Ottawa's population grew by three and a half times to allow the nation's capital to overtake Winnipeg, which slumped to Canada's fifth-largest centre by 1971. The establishment of a large federal bureaucracy after the Second World War was the main factor behind Ottawa's dynamism.

The following decade, Winnipeg slipped another two spots to No. 7 in Canada, as both Calgary and Edmonton experienced explosive growth during the oil boom of the 1970s. Finally in 2001, Winnipeg sunk behind Quebec City to the No. 8 position, where it remains today. And if current trends continue, Winnipeg will slip to No. 9 by the year 2021, behind Hamilton, Ontario.

The net effect of all this slow growth means that up until the new millennium, Winnipeg was spared the development pressures that have played havoc with urban development over the past fifty years in faster-growing Toronto, Vancouver and Calgary. Instead of flattening heritage structures, Winnipeg simply left its old buildings alone. But the lack of growth also meant many Winnipeg property owners felt little need to improve and maintain old warehouse and office buildings. So when a new business desired space, it was cheaper to build outside downtown than renovate in the inner city,

where heritage structures by and large were left alone.

At the same time, the combination of new heritage-conservation regulations, federal building codes and fire-safety standards made it expensive to conduct any sort of renovations in older buildings. And property owners who took the leap of faith faced penalties in the form of higher property-tax assessments and bills.

So by the late 1990s, when the Exchange was declared a natural treasure, many of downtown's most important and impressive structures were empty and in a sorry state. The Canadian Bank of Commerce building, a key component of Main Street's Bankers Row, did no more banking by 1969. Donald Street's Metropolitan Theatre, originally a luxury movie house, went dark in 1987. The Union Bank Tower, western Canada's first steel-frame skyscraper, had only pigeons for tenants after 1992. The Avenue Building, a Portage Avenue commercial edifice, lost all of its tenants by 1999. The Ashdown Hardware building, a key part of the Bannatyne streetscape since 1905, stood in imminent danger of being torn down shortly after the turn of the millennium.

Yet all of these structures are still standing today, by virtue of simply lasting long enough to see a day when Winnipeg regained just enough affluence and pride to sink serious money into heritage conservation. During the first decade of the twenty-first century, an unprecedented combination of private investment and government spending was funnelled into heritage restoration, renovation and reconstruction — sometimes just to preserve facades of buildings too far gone to actually save.

Almost a century of slow growth allowed all this wondrous architecture to avoid the attention of developers. Decades of neglect allowed much of it to begin crumbling. And in only a few short years of frenetic desperation, some of downtown's key structures were saved.

But don't go awarding Winnipeg a badge of heritage-conservation honour just yet, for the city also stood by and did nothing for many structures that were not deemed beautiful enough, important and convenient enough to preserve. You only have to step one metre outside the official boundaries of the Exchange to see what true neglect looks like. But that's a rant for another chapter. ■

The Johnston Terminal Building, one of Winnipeg's largest warehouses, rose on the south side of CN Rail's East Yards in 1928, right before The Depression seized the continent. It was vacant by 1977, as new yards outside the city made CN's downtown facilities obsolete. The four-storey freighthouse reopened in 1993 as the second main structure at The Forks — a home for restaurants and shops.

Two lots over from the Royal Albert Arms, the three-storey St. Charles arose the very same year at the corner of Notre Dame Avenue and Albert Street. Like the Albert, it too started off upscale, became decrepit and eventually housed an important music venue in the 1980s: Wellingtons, a basement venue with a stainless-steel dancefloor that became dangerously slippery after the first spill of beer. Despite a half-hearted effort to convert the St. Charles into a boutique hotel, it stands vacant and has an uncertain future.

LEFT / In 1871, James Ashdown started selling hardware at the northeast corner of Bannatyne Avenue and Main Street. An aggressive entrepreneur, he built a massive warehouse east of Main Street in 1895 and by the next decade had enough power to influence decisions at city hall, where he served one year as mayor. After an expanded version of his original hardware store burned in 1904, he used the same foundation as a base for a six-storey building whose original brick façade was obscured by later renovations. At the turn of the millennium, the mostly vacant building was once again threatened, this time by demolition. After a heated debate at city hall, a renovation that restored the original exterior gave the block new life as the Crocus Building, now home to offices for the Winnipeg Folk Festival, Winnipeg's Contemporary Dancers and the Manitoba Conservatory of Music. The Crocus name remains, despite the ignominious demise of the Crocus Investment Fund, an ill-fated labour-sponsored venture-capital corporation.

FAR LEFT / The cobblestone-paved vehicle tunnel beneath CN Rail's main line has been preserved in the form of Forks Market Road, which connects The Forks with the rest of downtown.

LEFT / The Canadian Bank of Commerce was an important component of Main Street's "Bankers' Row" when it was completed in 1911. It was vacated in 1969, when the Canadian Imperial Bank of Commerce moved into the Richardson Building at Portage & Main. After a push to demolish the building, philanthropist Bill Loewen spearheaded renovations and the old bank reopened in 2002 as the Millennium Centre. The lobby area now serves as a venue for weddings.

RIGHT / While some of the Exchange District's old warehouse structures succumbed to the wrecking ball, four buildings from the 1880s managed to survive in a row on Princess Street, west of the Civic Centre campus. Only their facades could be saved when Red River College incorporated them into a downtown campus later named The Roblin Centre. The adaptive reuse of the block not only saved the facades, but brought students downtown and served as a genuine catalyst for more development.

Don't be dismayed by the stark rear view: The Bell hotel is a success story on a strip of Main Street ravaged by decay, demolition and rush-job revitalization. Starting in the 1990s, the city and downtown development agency CentreVenture embarked on a two-decade demolition binge on the Main Street strip, mainly to eradicate low-end hotels with alcohol-and-drug-addicted occupants. This effort sent homeless and quasi-homeless people staggering into other areas of downtown. A remorseful CentreVenture purchased the Bell, originally built in 1906, and helped convert it into a housing-first apartment building, where people at risk of homelessness are given a room and supports even if they continue to drink or abuse substances. It reopened in 2011 and serves as a model for further conversions that may ease Winnipeg's housing crisis.

When the Allen Theatre opened on Donald Street in 1919, Winnipeg already had vaudeville houses like the Walker Theatre and Pantages Playhouse. What soon became the Metropolitan screened movies for almost eight decades before the venue went dark in 1987. Ironically, its sole use over the ensuing 25 years was to serve as a movie site. It finally reopened in 2012 after an $18-million restoration by the Canad Inns Hotel chain, which added a modern kitchen facility to the south of the building and hopes to take advantage of traffic from the MTS Centre.

Less than a decade after moving on to Princess Avenue, Red River College set its sights on the 10-storey Union Bank Tower, Western Canada's first steel-frame skyscraper — and the oldest surviving structure of its kind in Canada. Prior to steel-frame construction, building height in North America was limited by the load-bearing capacity of thick stone walls; the emergence of taller buildings in New York City and Chicago initially inspired skepticism. The Union Bank Tower was Winnipeg's signature piece of architecture when it opened in 1904. By 1992, when the Royal Bank of Canada moved out, it was vacant and in danger of dereliction. After a $35-million makeover that included the annex pictured here, it reopened in 2013 as Red River College's Paterson GlobalFoods Institute, with restaurants on the main flood, teaching kitchens and classrooms above it and student residences on upper floors.

8 THINGS WE DESTROYED

During the unpleasant final years of its 115-year existence, the Leland Hotel stood vacant and derelict at the corner of King Street and William Avenue. Given Winnipeg's embarrassment of heritage buildings, there was nothing all that unusual about a four-storey wood-and-brick structure sitting unused in the Exchange District. But the Leland sat immediately opposite William Avenue from city hall, only metres from the council chamber.

In 1995, the city purchased the Leland Hotel, but politicians never agreed to protect it. Built in 1884, it was once one of the city's most luxurious hotels. But decades of neglect had resulted in its abandonment, as no one could afford to do much with it. Official heritage protection was never granted to the Leland, despite some concern it ought to be saved. An arsonist finally settled the issue in 1999 by torching the cursed structure, rendering any future debate irrelevant.

After the death of an animal, it doesn't take long before flies and worms and other organisms come to devour the organic matter. When a building goes down in Winnipeg, the clean-up crews arrive even earlier to remove any trace of the remains. John K. Samson, who wrote the foreword to this book, was struck by the sudden emptiness of the Leland site when he wandered past it. That impression is immortalized in the first few lines of Left & Leaving, a song recorded in 2000 by John's band, The Weakerthans:

> My city's still breathing (but barely, it's true)
> Through buildings gone missing like teeth

More than a decade later, there are a lot of missing teeth in downtown Winnipeg. Despite Winnipeg's economic resurgence, stability and optimism after the turn of the millennium, buildings continue to burn down, get torn down or even fall down on their own.

That in itself is unfortunate. But what happens after the tooth is knocked out is even worse. The empty gap that remains turns out to be a highly profitable expanse of nothing for a property owner lucky enough to come into possession of a surface parking lot.

As of late 2010, downtown Winnipeg had no less than 154 surface-parking lots, almost all of which used to be buildings of some sort. The smallest can only hold a couple of cars. The largest has space for 600. Together, they represent 2.4 million square feet of empty downtown space worth no less than $100 million and likely many times more.

Three in ten of these lots are owned by some level of government or quasi-governmental agency. The rest are privately owned. All are very profitable to maintain as empty surface lots because there are no incentives in Winnipeg for property owners to build them up. Likewise, there are no penalties in Winnipeg for leaving the obnoxious expanses of nothingness alone.

Motorists who don't like to visit downtown claim there's nowhere to park in the middle of Winnipeg. What they really mean is there is nowhere to park for free downtown. From the vantage point of a seagull or hot-air balloon, Winnipeg's core looks like a sea of parking lots. On evenings and weekends when the Jets are not playing at MTS Centre, the vast majority of those lots are mostly empty. All that space exists so people can park from 9 to 5 p.m., Monday to Friday, in the neighbourhoods most easily reached by public transit.

Scale out that aerial view to a satellite level, and you'll see even more surface parking. Strip malls alongside regional streets, shopping malls in decentralized commercial districts and the big-box "power centres" in newer suburbs all gleam with masses of concrete, mainly because city zoning rules

The cracked pavement of a surface-parking lot off Smith Street places the towers of Winnipeg's financial district in the perspective they deserve.

demand every business to have a certain number of parking spots.

Motorists may consider these stalls free, but property owners pay for the additional square footage in the form of taxes. Those costs are then passed on to consumers in the form of higher prices. There really is no such thing as a free parking spot, even in a city where motorists will idle in traffic or circle blocks several times just for a crack at saving a loonie or two on the short-term rental of an automobile-sized stretch of asphalt.

Of course, there are other costs associated with surface-parking lots. Almost every drop of rain that winds up on concrete is carried away into the city's drainage system, which is already overtaxed by spring floods and the occasional intense summer rainstorm. This surface runoff carries petrochemicals, heavy metals and antifreeze into a wastewater-treatment system that wasn't designed to scrub inorganic environmental contaminants from the effluent it discharges into the Red River.

Surface parking lots also absorb more of the sun's energy than buildings or vegetation, creating islands of heat that actually combine to raise the entire temperature of the city, even during the depths of January. Ironically, empty lots also contribute to the windswept-tundra character of downtown thoroughfares such as Main Street on days when Winnipeg pedestrians could actually use a few extra degrees of warmth.

Surface lots also make people feel unsafe. Because there's so little activity on a surface lot, no one ever chooses to walk alongside one at night, if they have any alternative. Downtown's plethora of surface parking is particularly oppressive for pedestrians coming off late shifts. Parkades may not appear much safer, but at least they represent a more efficient use of space.

Perhaps the most disturbing facet of the surface parking lot is their curious ability to perpetuate themselves. In newer areas of Winnipeg, the creation of any new empty space reduces the city's density, making it even more difficult to get from one place to another on foot. And that means more people need cars, which require parking, which necessitates the need for more surface lots.

There are relatively easy solutions to ending this cycle. Zoning rules can be changed to eliminate requirements for a minimum number of parking spaces. Tax incentives can be offered to property owners who develop their surface lots. Penalties can be levied against those who do not. Government agencies can be directed to sell more valuable empty tracts, on the condition they are developed. And heritage-conservation policies can be enforced more vigorously to ensure property owners maintain their blocks.

The story of the Leland Hotel, meanwhile, has a happy little epilogue. Red River College's restoration of the Union Bank Tower included the construction of a three-storey annex on the Leland Hotel's old footprint.

That annex opened in 2013, almost 130 years after the Leland set up shop. The city's still breathing and may relax long enough to exhale. ◼

From Portage & Main, Winnipeg's
most important intersection,
you only have to walk 90 metres
to find a surface-parking lot.
This empty patch of Main Street
asphalt taunts the edifices of
Bankers' Row. As this book went
to print, a new tower was proposed
for the site.

Trappist monks left France in 1892 to establish a monastery along
La Salle River in St. Norbert, on the southern fringe of Winnipeg,
completing a brick-and-Tyndall stone structure by 1904. The monks
supported themselves for decades by selling honey, cheese and meat,
but left for Holland, Man. in 1978 to avoid the noise and increasing
traffic of the city. Five years later, vandals lit the vacant monastery
on fire. Happily, the stabilized ruins are now protected by a
provincial heritage park and are home to summer performances
by theatre troupe Shakespeare In The Ruins.

RIGHT / The Odeon Drive-In theatre in Headingley could hold as many as 1,000 vehicles at a time. After a 44-year run, it closed in 2008, long after the living room replaced the passenger vehicle as the ideal place for movie-watching and awkward teenage sex.

LEFT / The Starland Theatre stood on Main Street from 1911 to 2008, when it was demolished to make room for a Winnipeg Regional Health Authority facility. The nearby Epic Theatre was also torn down to make way for the bland WRHA edifice.

LEFT / Transcona Meats stood on Regent Avenue until 2010, when a demolition crew working without a permit led the building to collapse on to the sidewalk. An investigation revealed there were no safety measures in place and the wreck was full of asbestos.

RIGHT / The Annex to Lombard Avenue's Grain Exchange Building was added in 1920 and remained structurally sound until the day it was demolished in 2010. In was replaced by an alleyway to serve the Grain Exchange and a faux-heritage façade that conceals a small parkade. Go ahead and call it a Potemkin streetscape.

LEFT / In 1911, the Ontario Wind Engine and Pump Co. built a four-storey warehouse at the foot of the Arlington Bridge. Later occupants included Winnipeg Hydro, Regal Furniture and the brewer Minhas Creek, which demolished the building in 2011 with the promise of building a brewery on the site.

BELOW / During the dark days of the 1980s, when Winnipeg's music scene suffered from a lack of venues, the Blue Note Café on Main Street served as a crucial incubator of artistic talent. The venue's house band became the Crash Test Dummies, Neil Young briefly named his band The Bluenotes after a visit and former co-proprietor Mark Riddell tried to convince city hall to convert the site into an outdoor ampitheatre. Instead, it's a musical graveyard: The one-storey structure was demolished in 2011.

FAR LEFT / The Jermyn Building went up on Logan Avenue in 1908 and burned down in 2011. These are the remains of the day.

125

The Yellow Warehouse stood on Main Street for more than century, despite a fire that killed seven people — including two firefighters — only two years after the brick building opened in 1910.

THE YELLOW
NEW & U...
RESTAURANT EC...
...VES·FRIDGES·DISHES·CHAIR...
...E FIXTURES ETC.
IF YOU DON'T SEE "ASK" WE MAY HAVE IT
JAEN SIGN

GOOD FOOD
LOW PRICES

BREAKFAST SPECIALS
$2.25-$5.50

LUNCH SPECIALS
$3.95-$5.95

HomeMade
BURGERS & FRIES

TAKE-OUT 947-53...

BREAKFAST SPECIA...
BURGERS·FRIES·SO...

Ham-N-Eggs Grill offered up bargain-priced breakfasts on Princess Street since the 1950s in a low-slung block that already had a 40-year presence in the Exchange District. The diner was torn down in late 2011 to make way for multi-family housing.

The old passenger terminal at Richardson International Airport was completed in 1964 as part of a nation-wide effort to show off cutting-edge architecture and design. The glass-and-steel structure boasted custom-designed furniture and massive artworks that covered the north and south interior walls. In the eyes of many architects, it was the most impressive modernist structure in the city. The Winnipeg Airports Authority demolished it in 2012, citing the absence of a viable business plan to maintain the cavernous structure.

LEFT & BELOW / Although only a modest commercial building, the Albert Street Business Block was an important piece of the Exchange District streetscape for almost 90 years. The three-unit building encompassed the remains of a house built in 1877, surrounding by storefronts added in 1924. Beginning in 2007, the owner of the neighbouring St. Charles hotel made the first of several attempts to seek permission to demolish the block for the purposes of expanding the surface-parking lot behind it. That effort was rendered irrelevant after a fire gutted the block in 2012.

The sad story of the Shanghai Restaurant Building is emblematic of Winnipeg's unwillingness to preserve important streetscapes. Originally known as the Robert Block and later the Coronation Block, this two-storey mixed-use building arose on King Street in 1883 and served as offices for Winnipeg's mayor and council when the city's Victorian "gingerbread" city hall was under construction. Starting in the 1940s, it housed the Shanghai Restaurant, one of the city's first Chinese-Canadian restaurants and most certainly its longest serving. By the 1970s, neglectful owners failed to heat the upper level, resulting in water damage that was used to justify the 2012 demolition of the building. In an infuriating display of enabling bad behaviour, city council allowed the Chinatown Development Corporation to tear down the building even through the organization had yet to raise the money or develop plans for seniors housing that would replace it. It is now an empty lot in a Chinatown full of empty lots.

For six decades, the Canadian Football League's Winnipeg Blue Bombers played out of the Polo Park venue originally known as Winnipeg Stadium. The open-air venue had 12,000 seats when it opened in 1953. A series of renovations expanded the capacity up to 33,000 and then back down to 29,500 for its final years, when it was known as Canad Inns Stadium. Winnipeg football fans had a love-hate relationship with the asymmetric venue, which had lousy concessions, buttocks-freezing metal benches for seats in the upper decks and men's washrooms where open troughs acted as urinals. It was replaced in 2013 by Investors Group Field, the Bombers' new home at the University of Manitoba's Fort Garry campus.

9 PLACES OF WORSHIP AND INDOCTRINATION

Most of the world's monotheistic religions have some conception of a messiah, a leader anointed with the ability to liberate the populace and usher in an age of peace and happiness. Often but not always, the messiah is a divine figure whose emergence will mark a turning point in history.

In Zoroastrianism, a divinely conceived human saviour named Saoshyant will make the world perfect and immortal. In Judaism, the messiah will be the "son of David," an otherwise ordinary human being. In Christianity, the saviour is Jesus, the "son of God" martyred some time between 29 and 33 A.D. In Sunni Islam, he is The Mahdi, a human redeemer who may or may not be a descendent of the prophet Muhammad. In the largest branch of Shia Islam, The Mahdi is the Twelfth Imam, a leader hidden away from the world since 874 A.D. In the Bahá'í Faith, founder Bahá'u'lláh was born in 1817 and dreamt of uniting the world before he died in 1892.

At the risk of upsetting the faithful of all the world's great religions, Winnipeg only has one true faith. The messiah arrived in the Red River Valley in the form of a National Hockey League franchise whose return in 2011 provoked a public outpouring of emotion rarely seen inside any church, mosque, gurdwara, synagogue or temple.

The most traumatic event in Winnipeg's recent history was the loss of the original NHL Jets, who played their final game — a 4-2 first-round playoff loss to the Detroit Red Wings — on April 28, 1996. Born in 1972, the Jets played seven seasons in the World Hockey Association and seventeen more in the NHL. Beginning in the 1980s, majority owner Barry Shenkarow warned the club could not remain profitable playing out of the city-owned Winnipeg Arena, where the team had to pay rent and had no access to revenue from concessions and parking. By the 1990s, Shenkarow's predictions had come true, thanks to rising player salaries and a crippling Canada-US dollar exchange rate. In 1995, Shenkarow announced plans to sell the club, sparking public rallies to "Save the Jets" as well as an arena-building fundraising campaign that saw children break into their piggy banks.

All those pennies and nickels, however, could not finance the construction of a new downtown arena without the support of Winnipeg's corporate leaders, who viewed the investment as a dumb move considering the future prospect of even higher NHL player salaries. The Jets played one final season at Winnipeg Arena in 1995-96. After the loss

The Granite Curling Club, Manitoba's oldest and most venerated curling club, built its current home on the north bank of the Assiniboine River in 1912. The club was founded in 1880 by early curlers who preferred granite rocks to iron stones. Winnipeg regards itself as the curling capital of the world, a title disputed by both Edmonton and Bemidji, Minn.

to Detroit, the club left Winnipeg for the Sonoran Desert and became the Phoenix Coyotes.

For the next fifteen years, Winnipeg hockey fans wandered in a desert of their own, angry the National Hockey League allowed their unprofitable and unaffordable club to leave town. Since many Winnipeggers derived much of their sense of place from the profile afforded by the Jets, living in a city without an NHL club was disorienting and disturbing. The loss of the Jets was also a psychological blow to Winnipeggers who didn't even care about hockey, given the vague cultural memory of the city's past importance on the national stage. To some younger Winnipeggers, the NHL's departure marked the end of hope.

As a result, the mid-1990s were the darkest days for the psyche of a city that started to understand its glory days really were over. After the shock, denial and grief came the proverbial acceptance. And just like a human being, Winnipeg got over itself and finally started growing comfortable within its own medium-sized skin.

In 1997, the harrowing but successful flood fight gave the city a sense of purpose. In 1999, the Pan Am Games brought more people by the thousands and a new riverside ballpark to The Forks. The turn of the millennium saw a renewed national recognition of Winnipeg's cultural scene, which flourished in the absence of the NHL. And in 2004, the construction of MTS Centre on Portage Avenue created a venue that could house an NHL team, despite the presence of only 15,004 seats — the smallest capacity of any NHL rink.

The arena's owner, True North Sports & Entertainment, initially brought the American Hockey League's Manitoba Moose to town. Company president Mark Chipman then quietly set about courting the NHL, establishing a relationship that almost allowed the struggling and near-bankrupt Coyotes to return to Winnipeg in 2010.

The messianic return of the National Hockey League to Winnipeg was finally announced the morning of May 31, 2011. With the help of partner David Thomson, one of the world's richest men, True North purchased the Atlanta Thrashers and moved the club to Canada, where hockey really is a religion.

Even after the initial honeymoon, the Jets continue to dominate the cultural life in Winnipeg, only slightly edging out the community obsession with the Winnipeg Blue Bombers, the Canadian Football League franchise founded as the Winnipeg Football Club in 1930.

In 1935, the Winnipeg club — then known as the Winnipegs — became the first football club from western Canada to win the Grey Cup, the national championship. The club was then redubbed the Blue Bombers and grew in popularity to the point where demand for seats exceeded the capacity of Osborne Stadium, which stood on the site of the Great-West Life Assurance campus. In 1954, the Bombers moved to Winnipeg Stadium at Polo Park and remained until 2012. After winning 10 Grey Cups by 1990, the club's futility over the next few decades only compounded the sense of pro-sport hopelessness created by the loss of the Jets. At least the Winnipeg Goldeyes, the minor-pro baseball club owned by Mayor Sam Katz, won an American Association championship in 2012.

Now if you're tempted to take issue with the equation of professional sport with religion, just consider the volume of public funds that wind up in stadiums and arenas, the temples of our time. Investors Group Field, the Bombers' new home at the University of Manitoba, cost $201 million, all of it financed up front by the province. The $133.5-million

In 2013, the Winnipeg Blue Bombers moved into Investors Group Field, a 33,500-seat stadium at the University of Manitoba's Fort Garry campus. The $201-million stadium was created to provide new revenue streams for the non-profit football club. But changes to the construction plan ended up saddling the club with $95 million worth of loans, which should be repaid in time to build a new stadium.

price tag for MTS Centre included $40.5 million worth of contributions from Ottawa, Broadway and Main Street. Approximately $9 million of the $16-million tab for Shaw Park, where the Goldeyes play, came from the public purse.

Professional sport is not just a distraction in North America. Its devotees pay as much attention to its myriad scores, standings and statistics as Talmudic scholars used to pore over interpretations of Jewish scripture. When Noam Chomsky called sports "the new opiate of the masses," he was simply arguing American football has taken over from religion. Traditional places of worship, meanwhile, are just as often attended out of duty as they are out of love.

The first attempts to build churches in the Red River settlement were stymied by the same quasi-biblical forces that threaten all Winnipeg buildings — flood and fire. The first Catholic church of St. Boniface, a log chapel raised in 1818, was destroyed in the flood of 1826. Of four separate cathedrals that followed, two were destroyed by fire. The fifth St. Boniface Cathedral, completed in 1971, incorporates the walls and ruins of its predecessor.

The civic importance of the church cannot be overstated in Winnipeg, as religious institutions founded most of the city's hospitals and all of its universities. Father Norbert Provencher, the same man behind the first Catholic chapel, founded St. Boniface College in 1818. The Anglican Church founded St. John's College, predecessor to the University of Manitoba, in 1866. Grey Nuns started St. Boniface Hospital in 1871. The Presbyterian-founded Manitoba College (1871) and Methodist-founded Wesley College (1888) formed the eventual basis for the University of Winnipeg. The Salvation Army founded Grace Hospital in 1890 and Misericordia

Sisters founded their eponymous hospital in 1898. Mennonites founded Concordia Hospital in 1928 and the forerunner of Canadian Mennonite University in 1947.

Another key force in the development of the city was the ethnic community centre, which originally took the form of fraternal societies aimed at supporting new arrivals from Europe. After the turn of the twentieth century, Polish, German, Ukrainian, Belgian and Scandinavian clubs, among others, were both social institutions as well as beneficial societies in railway-boom Winnipeg. But the arrival of prohibition to Manitoba in 1916 slammed the lid on above-board alcohol consumption.

While prohibition only lasted five years in Winnipeg, the city has been trying to recover ever since. The city's first bars were only open to white men and did not allow standing, singing or any fun of any sort. Mid-century reforms allowed in women, people of indigenous descent, music and eventually dancing. But a confusing mess of liquor licenses, which granted inspectors responsibility for everything from monitoring sanitation to scrutinizing menus to approving entertainment, hampered the vibrancy of Winnipeg's nightlife for decades.

Not coincidentally, Winnipeg's love of sport helped fuel a reform of alcohol regulations, as the return of the Jets sparked an increase in downtown alcohol consumption on game day. At the same time, the city tried to clamp down on public intoxication outside the long-term apartment buildings that masquerade as hotels. One of the strategies involved the outright purchase of lower-end hotels where the downtrodden residents are in legitimate need of salvation — the genuine variety, that even the power of professional hockey cannot provide. ■

LEFT / The Winnipeg Goldeyes of the American Association of Independent Professional Baseball play at Shaw Park. The riverside ballpark was known as Canwest Park prior to the 2009 dissolution of the Canwest media conglomerate founded by the late Izzy Asper, a lawyer, politician, entrepreneur and philanthropist. The Canadian Museum for Human Rights, a more substantial aspect of Asper's legacy, hovers over right field.

BELOW / MTS Centre, home of the Winnipeg Jets, opened on Portage Avenue in 2004. Wedged into the former site of the Eaton's department store, the Phone Booth only seats 15,004 for hockey. After a 15-year absence from Winnipeg, the NHL's return in 2011 was greeted with a passion that ranged from rhapsodic to messianic.

ABOVE / It's tempting to say M.C. Escher designed the Administration Building at the University of Manitoba. But he was only 15 when it opened in 1913, and would have gotten lost had he attempted to navigate that staircase.

RIGHT / Taché Hall, a former residence at the University of Manitoba, opened in 1911, when the concept of "frosh week" remained in its infancy.

The original Isbister School rose on Vaughan Street in 1899. It's now part of the Winnipeg Adult Education Centre, which offers literacy classes and high-school courses to people over 18.

140

St. Boniface Hospital, the first in western Canada, predates the creation of City of Winnipeg by two years. Grey Nuns founded the hospital as a four-bed facility in 1871. It now sprawls along the east bank of the Red River, opposite The Forks.

LEFT / Deer Lodge Centre in St. James opened in 1916 to help soldiers recover from the First World War. It remains a rehabilitation centre, as well as a personal-care home. The modern wing in the middle was added in 1989.

BELOW / St. Boniface architect Étienne Gaboury's conical design for Precious Blood Church — formally, L'Eglise Precieux-Sang — evokes the Assiniboine tipis that once dotted southern Manitoba. The church is hidden away on Rue Kenny, a side street in St. Boniface.

Salem Mennonite
Brethren Church does
the prairie gothic thing
in the inner-city
neighbourhood of
West Alexander. The church
has stood on Alexander
Avenue since 1905.

ABOVE / They take their murals seriously in Transcona.
This is Tabor Baptist Church on Madeline Avenue.

RIGHT / Jesus is always ready to ascend at St. Nicholas Ukrainian
Catholic Church on Bannerman Avenue.

RIGHT / The Fortune Block, at the corner of Main Street on St. Mary Avenue, dates back to 1878, when entrepreneur Mark Fortune was amassing a real-estate empire in Winnipeg. He died on The Titanic when the great ship sunk in 1912. The main floor is now home to Times Change(d) High & Lonesome Club, a roots-music venue modeled on the small live stages in Austin, Texas, one of the few North American cities as weird as Winnipeg.

BELOW / The opening of The Spectrum Cabaret in 1987 marked the start a live-music renaissance in a Winnipeg music scene that was dominated by cheesy cover bands for a decade. The venue changed ownership in the 1990s and is now known as The Pyramid.

LEFT / Provencher Boulevard is home to The Belgian Club and its curiously unilingual sign, which is neither in French nor Flemish.

The rear entrance to Johnny G's Restaurant & Bar, on McDermot Avenue in the East Exchange,
is adorned by the best wooden fire escape north of the Florida Keys.

A north-facing room at the Balmoral Hotel offers stunning views of the
Part Source outlet on the other side of Notre Dame Avenue.

*The adaptive reuse of old movie theatres is never an easy task. Yet the old
Kings Theatre, on Portage Avenue is now home to a skate-and-snowboard shop.*

*The Royal Manitoba Theatre Centre, at the corner
of Market Avenue and Rorie Street, opened in 1970
as part of Manitoba's centennial celebrations.
The modernist structure was part of the same
megaproject that built the nearby Centennial
Concert Hall, Manitoba Museum and Planetarium.*

Card-carrying Communists such Jacob Penner and Joe Zuken served as respected members of Winnipeg's city council from 1933 to 1983. Today, the party only retains pockets of support in the North End, including this home on Selkirk Avenue.

10 SUBURBIA!

At the risk of oversimplifying the broad spectrum of human civilization, there are three types of places people live. But only two are easy to define.

Rural land encompasses wilderness regions, agricultural zones and the small towns scattered around these areas. Cities are heavily built-up environments with a high density of commercial and residential development.

Suburbs are less dense than the cities they surround, but certainly more built up than the rural areas they swallow up. This imprecision may be due to a disjunction between the popular conception of a suburb as a residential area and the technical definition: a political entity outside of a city's formal boundaries.

The fuzzy nature of the suburb also stems from the fact nobody likes to admit they live in one. Unlike cities and rural areas, which are often if not always romanticized, suburbs are derided as dull, dismissed as inefficient and demonized as the cause of almost any ill, from greenhouse-gas emissions (all that driving!) to poor physical fitness (all that driving!) to an insularity that borders on agoraphobia (I've never actually met any of my neighbours!).

As of 2011, roughly two out of five Canadians lived in suburbs. Suburbanites also accounted for roughly half the overall non-rural population, with the other half living inside cities. That census year, no less than 13.2 million Canadians called suburbs home. It's safe to say the vast majority of them exhibited little shame about their choice of habitation.

Winnipeg, however, is a very unusual case, as most of its suburbs — that is, in the conventional, residential-area sense — are actually located within the boundaries of the city. Roughly nine out of every 10 residents of the Winnipeg Census Metropolitan Area live inside the boundaries of the city of Winnipeg, thanks to the 1972 amalgamation of the old, historic city with thirteen neighbouring suburbs — six cities, two towns and five rural municipalities.

Winnipeg is hardly the only Canadian city to amalgamate with its suburbs. The city of Toronto merged with five neighbouring municipalities to create "Megacity" in 1998. Ottawa amalgamated with eleven suburbs in 2000. Montreal swallowed up a whopping twenty-seven of its neighbours in 2002 — and then in idiosyncratically Quebecois fashion, later allowed fifteen of them to secede from the new entity.

But Montreal, Ottawa and Toronto still have large suburbs on their shoulders that lie outside their political

At ground level, cul-de-sacs are simply depressing. The symmetry of suburban layout is better appreciated from the air.

boundaries: Laval, Gatineau and Mississauga, to name a respective few. In contrast, the eleven municipalities that make up the Winnipeg CMA — places where more than half the working population commutes into the city — are predominantly rural in character. In 2013, 709,000 of the 782,000 people in the Winnipeg metro area actually lived inside the city proper. And that removes the entire rationale for demonizing suburbia.

Before Winnipeg's amalgamation, the city was beginning to experience a hollowing-out phenomenon better known as an "urban doughnut." In the 1960s, the population of the city proper was declining, which meant its tax base was also declining. But the suburbs were growing, increasing the overall number of people using city services and infrastructure. The old City of Winnipeg found this scenario unsustainable, arguing it was subsidizing its suburbs. The creation of Unicity in 1973 was intended to rectify the situation. "One with the strength of many," the newly enlarged city's motto, was intended to celebrate this unified sense of purpose.

In reality, it took decades after amalgamation for the city to provide equal levels of services such as transit, fire protection, health inspections and mosquito control for all areas of the newly expanded city. Even in 2013, some residential streets in the former Rural Municipality of Charleswood continue to use open ditches for drainage. Dozens of homes in the southern regions of the former City of St. Vital and the old Rural Municipality of Fort Garry continue to have no access to the city's water supply. "One with the strength of many" actually means "Some need the strength to haul in their water."

As well, the unification of the city with its suburbs did not magically erase the urban-planning headaches associated with low-density development. While the construction of new single-family homes contributed to the city's tax base after Unicity, the ceaseless expansion of low-density neighbourhoods had the same negative impacts on older areas of the city. Arithmetical increases in city property-tax revenue simply could not keep pace with exponential increases in the cost of delivering services and maintaining infrastructure.

In fact, most of Winnipeg's old suburbs no longer resemble the popular conception of a shiny new residential neighbourhood filled with cul-de-sacs and winding streets. At least some of the roads in all of Winnipeg's former suburbs are arranged in efficient, easy-to-service grid patterns. And many regional streets in the former suburbs — the first arteries to sport services that catered specifically to commuters in automobiles — are now lined with heritage remnants of the early automobile age.

In the 1950s and 1960s, even grocery stores, dry cleaners and motels caught the modernist design bug, erecting signage that reflected the graphic-design esthetic of the postwar era. Just like a walk through the Exchange District allows pedestrians to experience century-old architecture, a drive down Portage Avenue, Pembina Highway or Nairn Avenue can allow attentive motorists to relive the silver age of the automobile, when motels and drive-in restaurants flourished.

No one is supposed to like the suburbs, whose main cultural contribution to North America is the widespread proliferation of anomie. Every book and film about suburban life — from The Graduate to The Ice Storm to American Beauty — reinforces this idea.

But as a city of suburbs, Winnipeg cannot afford to loathe itself any more than it already does. Winnipeg must embrace its suburbs and strive to improve them. The alternative is unpalatable, not to mention unsustainable. ◼

While there's no way around urban sprawl's environmental footprint, developers are finding ways to innovate. Royalwood, a development carved out of land on the east side of the Seine River, utilizes living wetlands instead of conventional drainage ponds.

The Sage Creek development lies west of Lagimodiere Boulevard and south of Fermor Avenue. The homogeneity of these homes on Linmar Way is less apparent from this vantage point just outside the subdivision, along Dawson Road, a precursor to the Trans-Canada Highway.

RIGHT / The lights of Nairn Avenue tempt the weak among us with all manner of hedonistic excess.

LEFT / On Regent Avenue, Hi Neighbour Sam greets visitors to Transcona, once a village unto itself. Commissioned in 1968, the mascot's potential as a tourist attraction has never been fully realized, as there is no cannabis component to the annual Hi Neighbour Festival.

*RIGHT / In Garden City,
no one can hear you scream.
The Sears on McPhillips Street
and Leila Avenue awaits its
fate, much like the rest of the
department-store chain.*

*BELOW / One of the last of the
original Winnipeg drive-in
restaurants, Thunderbird
refused to budge when a
developer assembled land for
a Safeway at the corner of
Jefferson Avenue and
McPhillips Street.*

*FAR RIGHT / Hoar frost renders
the working-class Weston
neighbourhood that much
more beautiful.*

LEFT / The sun never sets on St. James. This bike-and-pedestrian path runs between Portage Avenue and Sturgeon Creek.

MIDDLE / Little boxes on Notre Dame Avenue: "And a blue one and a yellow one. And they're all made out of ticky tacky. And they all look just the same."

BOTTOM / Up close and personal with the Silver Heights Shopping Centre, the only place in Winnipeg where you can buy a cup of fair-trade coffee and a crossbow.

RIGHT / From this point on Portage Avenue, Portage la Prairie is only 45 minutes away. Dare to dream, Winnipeggers.

RIGHT / Pembina Highway's Capri Motel offers motorists a chance to relive the 1950s, one week at a time.

LEFT / Magic emerges when it snows on a Safeway parking lot on Main Street. This modernist gem was built in 1964.

At one point in the 1980s, St. Vital Hotel was known to locals as The Nightmare
On Ellesmere. The action at the beer vendor is much quieter these days.

164

ABOVE / Mike's General Store on St. Anne's Road harkens back to the days when two-dimensional Charlie Chaplins attempted to trip you, wherever you went.

LEFT / The start of a new day in Linden Ridge offers endless opportunities — if you read "opportunities" as "breakfast at the Kenaston Boulevard fast-food chain of your choice."

11

A RIVER
RUNS
THROUGH US.

**On the enormous and almost incomprehensible scale of geological time,
Winnipeg stands on some of the newest real estate on the planet.**

The earth is about 4.6 billion years old. It took another two billion years for the continents to congeal. The first vertebrates finally crawled onto that land 360 million years ago, eventually evolving into the first mammals, primates and hominids about 200, 60 and seven million years ago, respectively. Humans finally showed up about 200,000 years ago — and then waited another 190,000 years for Winnipeg to become somewhat inhabitable.

The city of Winnipeg stands in the middle of a floodplain at the bottom of a former glacial lake created by the remnants of an ice sheet that only retreated in full about 8,000 years ago. To call Winnipeg "dry land" is little more than a conceit. On the scale of hydrological time — itself a tiny fraction of geological time — this city sits on a soggy patch of clay that can just as fairly be described as wetland. Environmental historian Shannon Stunden Bower uses the term "wet prairie" to describe the Red River Valley, where

year-to-year variations in precipitation can muddle the conventional conception of "land" as something permanent and unchangeable.

The Cree, Assiniboine and other First Nations who travelled around this area for centuries understood the variability. Low river levels during the winter would allow cold-weather camps close to the water, where riverbanks afforded a measure of protection from the chilling winds. Summers were spent on higher ground. But when white guys from Europe showed up, they decided the best place to build a city was not just in the middle of this quasi-wetland, but right at the spot where two frequently flooding rivers meet.

The Selkirk Settlers arrived in the Red River Valley in 1812. They were sent scurrying to the highlands of Stony Mountain and Birds Hill in 1826, when the largest flood in recorded history covered almost all of what's now Winnipeg. Smaller

The Red River Floodway control apparatus.

but significant floods also swamped parts of Winnipeg in 1852, 1861, 1897, 1904, 1916 and 1948. Then came the most destructive deluge of all, the Great Flood of 1950, which forced more than 100,000 people to flee their homes. Vast tracts of St. Vital, Fort Garry, Fort Rouge and St. Boniface were inundated for weeks.

Recognizing Winnipeg's future depended on some means of protecting the city from its waterways, Premier Duff Roblin — a Red Tory whose grandfather was also a Manitoba premier — championed for the idea of building a floodway channel around Winnipeg. A visionary and a pragmatist, Roblin also expanded social and education services, granted Francophones rights originally sought by Louis Riel and planted the seed for Winnipeg's 1972 amalgamation. But he'll mainly be remembered as the guy who oversaw the 1960s construction of the Red River Floodway, which spared Winnipeg from more than a dozen deluges as well as untold billions worth of damages.

The forty-seven-kilometre floodway cost $63 million to complete in 1968 and another $665 million to expand in 2010. Together with a dam and reservoir on the upper Assiniboine River and an Assiniboine floodway channel into Lake Manitoba, the Red River Floodway saved Winnipeg from five deluges similar or greater in magnitude to the 1950 event. The 1979 spring flood was almost as massive as the 1950 event. The even larger "Flood of the Century" in 1997 almost did an end-run around the floodway by spilling into the La Salle River. Only a last-minute military effort to build a dike along the southern edge of the La Salle River drainage basin averted a catastrophe. Floods in 2006 and 2009 were less severe, but remained complicated by the hydrological chaos of continued agricultural drainage and ice jams. Finally, a 2011 flood presented a threat from the west, where the Assiniboine River — whose lower portion is actually perched above the level of the surrounding land — threatened to spill its banks in the most spectacular manner since 1974.

Only seventy-five kilometres west of Winnipeg, high drama played out on a once-obscure curve of the Assiniboine known as Hoop and Holler Bend, where provincial engineers cut into a dike to deliberately flood adjacent farmland. While Winnipeg itself was never threatened, flood forecasters feared the failure of dikes on either the Assiniboine River or its floodway into Lake Manitoba would result in catastrophic property loss. So the engineers went to work, conducting a hydrological experiment in real time, without actually knowing for certain what would happen to thousands of nearby homes. And the entire time this was going on Winnipeggers went about their ordinary middle-of-May business, mowing lawns and grilling hamburgers and worrying about mosquitoes.

The lesson learned in 2011 was the Red River Valley does not belong to people. The land is merely on loan to Winnipeg and its residents. Fears about the Assiniboine spilling its banks were warranted because that river has done so dozens if not hundreds of times over the last few millennia. During the most massive floods, the Assiniboine carved out new channels or switched back to old ones in an effort to empty itself as quickly as possible. In fact, the Assiniboine used to flow into the Red River at St. Norbert, not The Forks — the La Salle River is a remnant of an earlier course.

The Red has changed courses, too, blasting across the narrow necks of peninsulas during major flooding events

to flow in more direct lanes — and create new oxbow lakes. Winnipeg neighbourhoods such as Kingston Crescent, which rests on a peninsula in the middle of a meander, are destined to be destroyed by a monstrous flood some day. So are many of Winnipeg's riverfront homes, given how easy it is for the Red to erode the soft clay of its banks during ordinary floods.

Extraordinary events, however, are expected to arrive more frequently. Climate-change models have long predicted more extreme weather events will appear in midcontinental regions of the planet, making highly variable climates even more variable. That means an increased likelihood of not just floods, but tornados, blizzards, extreme summer heat, and the hurricane-like storms known as weather bombs. It may already be happening: During the seven-year span between 2005 and 2011, Winnipeg experienced four major floods.

Happily, humans are highly adaptive creatures. Our ability to improvise has allowed us to infest the surface of the entire planet. Winnipeggers, who already deal with variability, will figure out a way to handle even greater extremes.

But anyone who lives in the middle of a floodplain — at the bottom of an old lake, itself left behind by a glacier — must recognize the impermanence of their situation. Winnipeggers live on land that isn't always land, along rivers that have swollen into lakes and will eventually swell again. And that will happen no matter how many great feats of engineering are devised to channel away the waters that are trying to define the shape of this very new and still-impressionable place. ▪

When the Red River rises high enough to threaten low-lying Winnipeg properties, the Manitoba Floodway Authority may raise the gates the Inlet Control Structure at Courchaine Bridge. The control structure can divert as much as 140,000 cubic feet of water — volume equivalent to two Olympic-sized swimming pools — into the Red River Floodway every second. The artificial ditch on the east side of Winnipeg runs 47 kilometres before it empties into the Red River just north of Lockport. Ordered up by former Manitoba Premier Duff Roblin, the original floodway project cost $63 million by the time it opened in 1968. An expansion completed in 2010 cost an additional $665 million. The expense has been worth it, as the floodway has spared Winnipeg from catastrophic flooding in 1979, 1997, 2009 and 2011 as well as moderate spring or summer flooding on at least 18 other occasions. The province estimates the floodway has averted more than $10 billion worth of property damage. Unfortunately, hydrological engineering on this scale comes with consequences: operating the control structure creates a Red River backflow effect that swamps land situated upstream.

Tree trunks on the St. Boniface side of the Red River are submerged during a spring flooding event. Even after the completion of the Red River Floodway, the river has crested as high as 7.5 metres above its normal winter ice levels. In Winnipeg, water levels are expressed in a given number of "feet James" — the height as measured by an automated monitoring device installed near the old James Avenue Pumping Station.

La Salle River, the most pristine of Winnipeg's four rivers, enters the Red River at St. Norbert. As recently as several hundred years ago, the lower portion of the Assiniboine River flowed along this channel. A course change during a catastrophic flooding event allowed the Assiniboine to carve out its present course. This placid stretch is inside La Barriere Park, near Winnipeg's southern edge.

The siltiness of the Red River belies its biodiversity. No less than 70 of the 95 species of fish found in Manitoba spend some or all of the year in the Red River. In Winnipeg, it's possible to catch excellent food fish such as walleye, sauger, yellow perch, northern pike, burbot and two species of catfish, the black and brown bullhead. The latter three are particularly tasty but extremely unappreciated, possibly because of the burbot's eel-like appearance and an irrational angling prejudice in Canada against eating any bottom-feeder with barbells.

Underutilized in the summer, the Assiniboine River may as well be a wilderness waterway during the winter months. Snowshoe and ski tracks reveal evidence of human existence on this stretch alongside Assiniboine Park.

RIGHT / Except for one whitewater stretch that emerges south of Portage Avenue during the spring snowmelt, Sturgeon Creek is a placid ribbon. The largest of Winnipeg's four official creeks begins west of the city before crossing into St. Charles and eventually spilling into the Assiniboine River in the neighbourhood of Woodhaven.

FAR RIGHT / Omand's Creek is a Frankenstein monster of waterway that includes the upper course of what used to be Colony Creek, an artificial channel that runs through the Polo Park area and a small natural creek that runs into the Assiniboine River in the Wolseley neighbourhood. The channel portion is overgrown during the summer alongside Westview Park, a green space better known as Garbage Hill. The former landfill is now the highest point in the city. The entire the West End is visible from its lofty summit.

Two generations of children have been frightened into good behavior by The Witch's Hut in Kildonan Park, erected alongside a short creek in 1970. The City of Winnipeg owned both Kildonan and Assiniboine Park even before the 1973 creation of Unicity. Before the amalgamation, the two parks existed as city reserves outside of its boundaries.

Within the boundaries of the City of Winnipeg, there are four rivers, four creeks and at least three dozen ponds or lakes, the vast majority of them artificial basins designed to store stormwater. The more naturalized basins, like this pond on the grounds of the Royal Canadian Mint, have enough vegetation to support fish, amphibians and insects and the waterfowl who prey on them. Blue herons, white pelicans, mallards, blue-winged teals, wood ducks, pintails, northern shovelers, goldeneye are common inside the city, while Canada geese number in the obnoxious tens of thousands.

177

ABOVE / The Assiniboine River, shortly before the freeze-up. Armstrong Point,
one of Winnipeg's oldest residential neighbourhoods, is in the foreground at left.
The condominiums on the opposite side of the river sit alongside Wellington Crescent.

RIGHT / In the midst of a winter storm, visibility can be reduced to a matter of metres.
Here, blowing snow obscures a road inside Assiniboine Park, the city's largest.

Downtown Winnipeg, struck by lightning once more.

12

THE MORE
THINGS CHANGE

To understand the character of a city, consider its first mayor. Winnipeg's founding leader was a drunk, violent, foul-tempered, Francophone-hating racist from Ontario who incited riots and effectively stuffed the ballot box to win the city's first election.

The man in question was Francis Evans Cornish, a London, Ontario lawyer who was elected mayor of his hometown despite a penchant for getting into fights. He was run out of office in London when other members of his council hired soldiers to ensure a fair election. After failing to win provincial office in Ontario, Cornish left his wife behind and made his way to Fort Garry, then capital of a province largely founded by the very people hated by Ontario Orangemen — the French-speaking, Catholic "half-breeds" known as the Métis.

Cornish made an immediate impression upon his arrival in 1872, a federal election year. Rallying other new arrivals from Ontario, Cornish ransacked a St. Boniface polling station in supposed protest of the fact he and his Anglo buddies hadn't lived in the Red River settlement long enough to vote. He also fired up a mob to attack police and break into the offices of newspapers they deemed unsympathetic to the Orange cause. He was also the prime suspect in a bizarre incident where the speaker of the Manitoba Legislature was waylaid en route to an

Listen to the Westbrook Hotel cowboy.
He knows of what he speaks.

appointment, dragged out of his carriage and then tarred in the middle of the street.

This stellar resume was all Cornish needed to make a run for office in his muddy adopted home. After leading the charge to have Winnipeg incorporated as a city, Cornish won the first mayoral race in 1874 by a margin of 383 to 179. This was fascinating considering there were only 388 registered voters at the time.

Cornish only lasted a single year in office, but has yet to be surpassed in terms of bad behaviour. Few Winnipeggers realize their city's first mayor was considered a violent extremist even by the standards of the late nineteenth century.

Pretty much all white people were racist at the time, when even progressive ethnologists believed societies passed through linear stages of development. The common belief, even among educated men and women, was that indigenous Canadians were primitive people who needed to adopt European customs in order to join so-called civilization. This mentality persisted well into the twentieth century in Manitoba in the form of a residential schools program that involved the abduction, re-education and often abuse of First Nations children.

For much of Winnipeg's existence, the city's indigenous population had little respect and even fewer rights. But the First Nations and Métis weren't alone — Winnipeg's early leaders had no time for other ethnic groups, either. The eastern Europeans who flooded into western Canada to help settle the prairies were initially hailed as hard-working farmers. But when tens of thousands of Ukrainian, Polish, German, Russian, Romanian, and other European immigrants settled in Winnipeg, they were ghettoized in the North End, deprived of the best of city services and derided as leftist

revolutionaries. In many ways, the 1919 general strike could be seen as a clash between the city's Anglo-Protestant elite and pretty much everyone else. Winnipeg's large German community also endured suspicion during both world wars. During the Second World War, German-born Canadians who came to Canada after 1921 were forced to register as "enemy aliens."

Winnipeg's attitudes toward anyone who wasn't of British extraction finally softened during the postwar period. The city's unofficial Anglo-Protestant hegemony finally ended in 1956, when the Ukrainian-Canadian Stephen Juba won Winnipeg's mayoral race. At the same time, changes in federal immigration policies allowed new ethnic groups to arrive. Italians, Greeks and Portuguese were among the wave of southern Europeans who moved to Winnipeg in the 1950s and 1960s. The 1970s and 1980s saw an upswing in immigration from Asia, with emigrants from the Phillippines, South Asia and China leading the way. Refugees from civil strife in Latin America, East Africa and Central Asia also arrived at the end of the cold war and into the new millennium, creating a truly multi-ethnic Winnipeg. By 2006, Statistics Canada recorded 203 different ethnic groups in Winnipeg, including a 90-member Mayan community, 45 Maoris from New Zealand and 20 Fulani from West Africa.

Winnipeggers, however, tend to exaggerate the diversity of the city and are fond of perpetuating the utter fiction that the city is the most multi-cultural centre in Canada. That may have been true in 1911, but it is far from the case by now, as Vancouver, Toronto, Montreal and even Calgary are far more diverse by any statistical measure you choose: country of origin, ethnicity, first language and visible-minority status.

In fact, Winnipeg remains a place where ethnic tensions run deep. They just no longer involve the English vs. French duality of the 1870s or the Canadian-born vs. immigrant strife of the early twentieth century. Rather, ethnic inequality in Winnipeg is now a question of indigenous citizens vs. everyone else, as the city's urban Aboriginal population continues to endure more poverty, more crime, less employment, more incarceration, less education, more health problems and less income, on average, than Winnipeggers of all other ethnic backgrounds. Systemic racism remains Winnipeg's greatest challenge, despite the reforms made in the aftermath of Manitoba's Aboriginal Justice Inquiry of 1988, the creation of beneficial institutions such as the Aboriginal Centre of Winnipeg in 1992 and a vast and concerted effort to otherwise improve the lives of the city's First Nations and Métis residents.

On top of this virtual apartheid, overt racism also remains, even without an extremist mayor like Cornish to inflame the most reactionary segments of the populace. To be indigenous in Winnipeg in the twenty-first century is to endure suspicion from people who are not indigenous. This is highly ironic, considering Winnipeg has the highest per-capita indigenous population of any city in North America. Roughly one in every nine Winnipeggers can claim some form of aboriginal ancestry.

The good news is the statistical gulf between Winnipeg Aboriginal and non-Aboriginal populations is closing. There is hope the near future will see an end to a socio-economic duality that breaks down along ethnic lines. Behind this hope is a simple matter of demography: indigenous Winnipeggers happen to be the fastest-growing segment of the city's population. Without the Aboriginal community and immigrants, the city would not be enjoying

On March 23, 1952, Winnipeg-born Chicago Blackhawks right-winger
Billy Mosienko scored three goals in 21 seconds against the New York Rangers.
The fastest-hat-trick record has stood ever since. Mosienko died in 1994.
The bowling lane that bears his name stands on Main Street, in the North End.

a modest resurgence, as those two subgroups account for almost all of the city's recent population growth.

The challenge for the city is to keep on growing, and not just by adding more streets and sewer pipes and subdivisions. Winnipeg must grow up, both in terms of adding density to existing neighbourhoods and adopting a more mature mindset. The city has survived economic overheating, a sudden recession and almost a century of slow decline. It has suffered from poor planning and short-sighted political decision-making. It has been wounded psychologically. Yet Winnipeg endures.

The city is blessed with the beauty of the winter sunshine, a summer elm canopy and year-round ribbons of water and ice. It boasts North America's largest intact collection of turn-of-the-twentieth-century architecture and some of Canada's most robust modernist structures. It possesses a passionate and creative populace, imbued with an unusually fierce form of collective identity.

Visitors to Winnipeg occasionally remark upon the cynicism of this populace, but what they're really encountering is the pragmatic, prairie version of idealism. World-weariness is the direct result of comparing the way things are to the way you want things to be. And Winnipeggers have never stopped dreaming, in spite of learning they must place parameters on the scope of those dreams.

Winnipeg may be stuck in the middle of a floodplain, at the centre of a continent. Winnipeg may be enveloped by a suffocating blanket of profound ambivalence. But Winnipeg is not stuck in time.

Winnipeg knows it can't regain the glory of the past any more than it can dictate the terms of the future. So Winnipeg exists in the moment, finally aware of both itself and its place in the world. ◼

ABOVE / The Canadian Grain Commission Building is the place you want to be if you think you have what it takes to regulate the way the nation handles cereal. This is no place for the weak, the timid or the triticale-averse.

BELOW / Spring is in the air on Canora Street, in Wolseley.

The magnificence of Lombard Avenue, betrayed by the absence of humanity. Some day soon, my friends. Some day soon.

LEFT / The Scott-Bathgate buildings on Westbrook Street may very well be Winnipeg's favourite warehouses. A downtown without the Can-D-Man just wouldn't be right.

BELOW / Situated across Notre Dame Avenue from the Health Sciences Centre, Roy's Florist has borne witness to more happiness and grief than just about anywhere else.

187

BELOW / *In 1900, Montreal's Gault brothers built an Arthur Street warehouse to store dry goods. It was converted seven decades later into studios for arts organizations as part of the Manitoba Centennial Centre project. Cinematheque, the repertory cinema, operates out of the first floor.*

RIGHT / *Don't be fooled by the open water: When it's this bright in Winnipeg in winter, it's freezing outside.*

ABOVE / The Manitoba Legislature grounds and downtown's Broadway-Assiniboine neighbourhood glow from a vantage point at One Evergreen Place in Osborne Village.

RIGHT / "There's no zoning like Winnipeg zoning — like no zoning I know! Everything about it is appealing! Everything the traffic will allow! Nowhere could you have that happy feeling! When you aren't raising someone's eyebrow!" Somehow, it's OK to build a commercial building on your lawn on Sherbrook Street.

RIGHT / The entrance to Omand Park, at the corner of Wolseley Avenue and Raglan Road, is precisely where the joggers wheeze after running up the short trail from the bottom of Omand's Creek.

BELOW / Advance Electronics, an independently owned retailer, continues to survive on Portage Avenue with only a handful of parking spaces and no Sunday shopping.

Pollock's Hardware on Main Street has whatever you need — provided it's insect repellent, a toy glider and a Zippo lighter. You never know when you'll have to light a mosquito-resistant airplane on fire.

LEFT / The Yale Hotel has stood on the Main Street strip since 1906. There's no looking back now.

RIGHT / As the Ellice Avenue mural explains, Winnipeg actor Adam Beach grew up playing baseball with polar bears before moving to Hollywood to scream about samosas in Navajo.

The Garrick Hotel, on Garry Street, in a city once known as Fort Garry.

The modular design of Centre Village, a 2010 attempt to redefine the idea of low-income housing, brings a whimsical touch to Balmoral Street in the city's core.

From this angle at sunset, downtown Winnipeg appears a mid-20th Century paradise. Unfortunately, only two of the structures in the frame are residential buildings.

*Humanity sets off in different
directions in Osborne Village.
Winnipeg's fate remains
unwritten. So long, folks —
it's been swell.*

SELECTED SOURCES

Ager, Milton and Jack Yellen. *Happy Days Are Here Again*. EMI Robbins Music Catalog/Advanced Music Corp, 1929

Canada's Historic Places. Federal-provincial online registry at *www.historicplaces.ca*

Cassidy, Christian. West End Dumplings. Blog entries at *westenddumplings.blogspot.ca*

City of Winnipeg. Heritage assessments, historical documents and other records at *www.winnipeg.ca*

Environment Canada. Climate data at *www.weatheroffice.gc.ca*

Deer Lodge Centre. History at *www.deerlodge.mb.ca*

Granite Curling Club. History at *www.granitecurlingclub.ca*

Heritage Winnipeg. Heritage Winnipeg Virtual Library. Documents at *www.virtual.heritagewinnipeg.com*

Keshavjee, Serena, ed. *Winnipeg Modern: Architecture, 1945-1975*. Winnipeg: University of Manitoba Press, 2006

Kives, Bartley. *A Daytripper's Guide to Manitoba: Exploring Canada's Undiscovered Province.*
    Winnipeg: Great Plains Publications, 2006 and 2010

Maddin, Guy and George Toles. *My Winnipeg*. IFC Films, 2008

Manitoba Historical Society. Articles and documents at *www.mhs.mb.ca*

Mann, Charles C. 1491: *New Revelations of the Americas Before Columbus*. New York: Knopf, 2005

Parks Canada. Documents at *www.pc.gc.ca*

Scott, Bryan. *Winnipeg Love Hate*. Winnipeg: Lone Capone Press, 2010

Siamandas, George. The Winnipeg Time Machine. Blog entries at *timemachine.siamandas.com*

St. Boniface Hospital. History at *www.sbgh.mb.ca*

Swan, Ruth. *Frank Cornish — The Man*. Manitoba Historical Society, Dec. 18, 2011, www.mhs.mb.ca

Statistics Canada. Census data at *www.statcan.gc.ca*

Stewart, Kenneth W. and Douglas A. Watkinson. *The Freshwater Fishes of Manitoba*. Winnipeg: University of Manitoba Press, 2004.

Stunden Bower, Shannon. *Wet Prairie: People, Land and Water in Agricultural Manitoba.*
    Vancouver: University of British Columbia Press, 2011

Taylor, Peter, ed. *The Birds of Manitoba*. Winnipeg: Manitoba Naturalists Society, 2003

Welsted, John, John Everitt, and Christoph Stadel, eds. *The Geography of Manitoba — Its Land and its People.*
    Winnipeg: University of Manitoba Press, 1996

The Canadian Press. New census data shows Canadian suburbs rule. April 11, 2012

Winnipeg Building Index. University of Manitoba online registry at wbi.lib.umanitoba.ca

Winnipeg Free Press. Electronic and physical archives, 1872–2013

ACKNOWLEDGEMENTS AND THANKS

Generally speaking, coffee-table books are for people who don't like coffee, tables or books. What you have in your hands right now is the end-result of an attempt to create an illustrated book free of undue reverence for its subject matter.

Many of the facts and figures in this book are derived from the City of Winnipeg's vast online treasury of heritage assessments, the University of Manitoba's Winnipeg Building Index, the *Winnipeg Free Press* archives and websites maintained by Statistics Canada, Heritage Winnipeg, Manitoba Historical Society, Parks Canada and other publications, both online and in print. Please see the Selected Sources section for a more complete listing.

This book would not exist without the patience and encouragement of Gregg Shilliday, Maurice Mierau, Mel Marginet, Catharina de Bakker, and Susie Moloney at Great Plains Publications and the work of Suzanne Braun's creative team at Relish New Brand Experience.

We could also fill several surface-parking lots with appreciation for all the patience, love and support offered by our respective spouses, Jennifer Upton and Katarina Kupca.

To John K. Samson, thank you for unwittingly planting the creative seed for this project and then graciously becoming a part of it. We must also credit the influence, encouragement and criticism offered by journalists, bloggers and agitators who've helped make Winnipeg a more interesting if not better place.

On an individual level, Bryan must thank his architecture and graphic-design instructors for teaching him how to see the world. He cites photographers Henry Kalen, L.B. Foote, John Paskievich, Fred Herzog and Vivian Maier as inspirations.

Bryan acknowledges his employer, Herman Bekkering, for his support during the development of this book and throughout his photography career, and all the people who have helped, commented and spread the word about Winnipeg Love Hate. Rod Sasaki warrants a special mention for displaying and promoting Bryan's work at Warehouse Artworks.

Finally, Bryan also wishes to thank his family and friends for all of their love and support.

Bartley must thank Sammy Kohn, who tried to sell him on the concept of a book called *Shitty Things* in the 1990s. A more tangible inspiration for this book arrived in the form of *Big Box Reuse*, a 2008 exploration of the landscape of consumerism, by Ohio multimedia professor and artist Julia Christensen.

Bartley owes an Ashdown Warehouse full of debt to everyone who purchased a copy of his first book, the media who promoted it and the bookstores that sold it. Without them, this tome would not exist.

As well, without the flexibility afforded by *Winnipeg Free Press* editors Paul Samyn, Scott Gibbons and Shane Minkin, Bartley would not have been able to complete the text for this book. Bartley also acknowledges the support of his family and the friends he ignored during the writing process. Finally, thank you to Kaitlin and Lynn Murphy for allowing us to honour the memory of their father, Michael Murphy.

May the city of Louis Riel and Frank Cornish live forever. And may the spirit of John Ferguson forever regret drafting Jimmy Mann.

Bartley Kives and Bryan Scott